PSYCHODY...

COUNSELLING IN ACTION

D0523966

Series Editor: Windy Dryden

Counselling in Action is a series of short, practical texts developed especially for counsellors and students of counselling. Each book in the series is the ideal introduction to a particular theoretical approach and offers clear guidelines for practice, emphasising in each case the actual process of counselling.

Many of the books are now regarded as classic texts and a fundamental part of many training courses. Sage is pleased to announce that new and expanded editions are now available.

New editions in the series include:

Feminist Counselling in Action, Second Edition
Jocelyn Chaplin

Gestalt Counselling in Action, Second Edition
Petrūska Clarkson

Transcultural Counselling in Action, Second Edition
Patricia d'Ardenne and Aruna Mahtani

Rational Emotive Behavioural Counselling in Action, Second Edition
Windy Dryden

Psychodynamic Counselling in Action, Second Edition
Michael Jacobs

Person-Centred Counselling in Action, Second Edition
Dave Mearns and Brian Thorne

Personal Construct Counselling in Action, Second Edition
Fay Fransella and Peggy Dalton

Transactional Analysis Counselling in Action, Second Edition
Ian Stewart

Standards and Ethics for Counselling in Action, Second Edition
Tim Bond

Psychosynthesis Counselling in Action, Second Edition
Diana Whitmore

PSYCHODYNAMIC
COUNSELLING

Second Edition

Michael Jacobs

SAGE Publications
London • Thousand Oaks • New Delhi

First published 1988
Reprinted 1989, 1990, 1991, 1992, 1993, 1994 1996, 1998

This second edition first published 1999. Reprinted 2000, 2001

SAGE Publications Ltd
6 Bonhill Street
London EC2A 4PU

SAGE Publications Inc
2455 Teller Road
Thousand Oaks, California 91320

SAGE Publications India Pvt Ltd
32, M-Block Market
Greater Kailash – I
New Delhi 110 048

British Library Cataloguing in Publication Data

A catalogue record for this book is
available from the British Library

ISBN 0 7619 6300 6
ISBN 0 7619 6301 4 (pbk)

Library of Congress catalog record available

Typeset by M Rules
Printed and bound in Great Britain by Biddles Ltd
www.biddles.co.uk

Contents

FOREWORD

It was the unique contribution of Freud, to show that psychological conflicts unresponsive to reason or reassurance had to be understood as the products of unconscious motives and feelings. As others took up his ideas, they invariably encountered a puzzling phenomenon. Despite even desperate needs to be free of distress, those who began to explore their inner worlds soon wanted to give up the endeavour. There would ensue, for instance, an illusory sense of well-being or a negativity to the therapist and his work. Understanding the origins of this resistance, and how it could be overcome, thus became a crucial feature in the training of those who sought to relieve painful conflicts in others. Indeed, without this training, it can be said that little or no effective change can be achieved.

Freud's contribution has been developed by many thinkers, both those adopting his basic assumptions and others who have followed lines that were in some measure independent. Thus the field of knowledge is today a very wide one, usually referred to as 'psychodynamic' to give it a broader connotation than that of 'psychoanalytic'. Michael Jacobs gives in this book an outstandingly valuable account of the counselling process when this is informed by psychodynamic understanding. From his wide-ranging studies he gives well-balanced sensitive appraisals with the result that he shows in a clear and attractive way how it is applied in practice. He dispels naive expectations of psychological conflicts being overcome with little effort.

Nevertheless, he brings out from the progressive nature of the process of understanding one's self, the substantial gains that may be made within feasible periods, gains that permit a more satisfying life and which can go on being added to if the individual wishes. He also does the important service of banishing unrealistic expectations that this process can be administered to a passive subject. Instead, the individual embarking on this task shares the responsibility for his own self-development in a partnership with his counsellor. It is an investment in potential resources that can bring a valuable return in the whole sense of being.

A common difficulty for writers in this field is to safeguard the identity of their clients. Michael Jacobs makes brilliant use here of a novel solution. He takes some emotional stresses of ordinary people as described from the acute observations of human nature of one of our great writers – Charles Dickens. From these he fashions imaginary 'case-histories' that are remarkably convincing as samples of the real thing. Readers who want to improve their counselling skills will be amply rewarded as will those who wish to learn what counselling involves. For all there will be a deeper understanding of human nature and an enriched appreciation of the great literature devoted to that aim.

John D. Sutherland CBE, FRCPsych
formerly Medical Director of the Tavistock Clinic

PREFACE TO SECOND EDITION

This is the fourth of my books which I have revised for a second edition. It has been the most straightforward to revise, and this has caused me to reflect on why this might be so.

I think by the time I wrote the first edition of *Psychodynamic Counselling in Action* I had developed a style with which I remain content. I have only altered a few phrases to improve the flow. I also find that for the most part what I wrote in 1988 remains as true and relevant for me in 1998. But there are some significant additions in this edition to which it is worth drawing attention:

1. I have extended the references, and the bibliography is much fuller and more up to date than before. It is my impression that this book is used on a number of post-graduate courses as well in some trainings for psychotherapy. The reader will therefore wish to know where to turn for further reading, and I hope I have supplied this in good, but not daunting, measure.

2. I have been compelled (not against my will) to recognise just how much counsellors are now working with clients who a few years ago would have been thought only suitable for highly experienced therapists or mental health professionals. What is encouraging is that these counsellors have proved themselves effective with this extended client group, and, I have to say, in some instances have shown up not only the paucity of therapy available to the general population, but also the unwillingness of some therapists to get engaged with difficult clients. I intend no slight on psychotherapy, but it is important to recognise just how much experienced

therapists and experienced counsellors have in common in their ability to work with complex cases.

3.   The attention given to the therapeutic relationship has developed in the last ten years, and I needed to take note of the different ways in which it is experienced in practice. I have myself extended Clarkson's five-relationship model, in a way that I think is constructive. It is this section (Chapter 6) where I have made the greatest changes, partly to order, partly to content.

There are few readers who will want to take a fine tooth-comb to the first edition and to compare it, in the manner of the textual critic, to the second. Were they to do so they will find many examples of subtle change of mood from indicative to subjunctive; they will spot a softening of my attitudes, and some appropriate weakening of my convictions. This may come with the mellowing of increasing age and experience; with the greater confidence of not knowing; and through being able to better tolerate uncertainty. But I think it is also a reflection of the way the best psychodynamic thinking is going. We no longer need to fight battles, and win over the minds of the sceptics. The psychodynamic approach is well established, and growing in relevance for trainees from other orientations. Psychodynamic counsellors can validly look for ways in which their ideas and practice may need to be qualified, or even to change.

Michael Jacobs
Leicester

PREFACE TO FIRST EDITION

A word of explanation is necessary about the case examples included in the main text. Given my brief, to write about the psychodynamic approach to counselling from start to finish, it seemed right to take the reader through two cases from beginning to end. This presented difficulties. Whereas case vignettes can be sufficiently disguised to prevent identification of the client, lengthier examples run the risk of giving away too much information. The alternative was to disguise them so much that they read more like a figment of the counsellor's imagination than the facts of a case. Furthermore, to alter identifying features is less easy than it sounds.

I chose instead to take two characters from Dickens, and to imagine that they had presented themselves to me, with some of the emotional difficulties which Dickens himself gives them. In fact, no sooner had they appeared on paper before me, and in dialogue with me within my mind, than they ceased to be creations of Dickens and became as much my own, although where possible I used events in their lives as they appear in the books. Dickens presented me with the dilemmas and most of the facts; I had to provide the counsellor! I had, however, to increase Little Nell's age to present a cogent twentieth-century picture; and, for similar reasons, to alter Doctor Manette from a French doctor, imprisoned in the Bastille, to an Eastern European refugee.

The danger was that I might use such fictions to idealise my approach, and so present perfect examples of technique. As it turned out, it was easier to record some of my own mistakes in relation to fictional characters than it would have been to clients who were still identifiable to me. As

I imagined Little Nell (now Hannah) and Doctor Manette (now Karl) before me, I introduced disguised examples of actual work with a range of clients, particularly where interactions in actual practice were similar to the counselling which my imagination was pursuing. There is nothing in the text that could not have been said in the course of one of my sessions; and the understanding which I brought to my two 'clients' reflects the thinking I would myself have done had they been 'real' people. Dickens did not provide the psychodynamic hypotheses!

But if Dickens did not do that, I found that he, like other great novelists, dramatists and poets who wrote before Freud, had anticipated many of Freud's insights. Anyone who doubts that Dickens prefigured Freud should read Part II, chapter nineteen of *A Tale of Two Cities,* where the explanation and the cure for Doctor Manette's shifts of personality are brilliantly described. Manette and Mr Lorry discuss whether the disorder of a man's mind could be renewed by studying too much. Doctor Manette replies, 'I do not think that anything but the one train of association would renew it . . . some extraordinary jarring of that chord . . .' Then Dickens writes: 'He spoke with the diffidence of a man who knew how slight a thing would overset the delicate organisation of the mind, and yet with the confidence of a man who had slowly won his assurance out of personal endurance and distress.' By my last chapter the reader will see how 'the one train of association' helps us to understand Karl. And sexuality and separation broods over Little Nell throughout *The Old Curiosity Shop*.

As in my previous writing, I owe much to the students with whom I work, in training and supervising them, for making me clarify the psychodynamic approach so that they, and indeed I, can understand it better. My wife, Valerie, goes on tolerating being a 'word processor widow', and I thank her for her love and patience with me when I am short temperedly trying to get the phrasing right.

My editor, Windy Dryden, can sometimes infuriate me as much as I do myself, with his detailed comments and corrections; but that is probably because we are similar characters, even if of different theoretical orientation! Because he was, however, so painstaking in asking what some of my sentences meant, and in requesting complicated passages to be made more intelligible, the reader who finishes this book with greater understanding will partly have him to thank, and will appreciate my own real and sincere gratitude to him.

Michael Jacobs
Tugby, Leicestershire

Introducing the

Psychodynamic Approach

An Important Question

Hannah perched cautiously on her chair as the session began. She looked out of the window for a second, then turned her head rapidly, and fixed me with a rather threatening gaze. 'Are you a psychoanalyst?', she said, her voice indicating the same feeling of anxiety that her body language had already communicated to me.

I paused a second, wondering if the sense which I had of being threatened reflected her own feeling. I waited just long enough to see if she wanted to say more, but she clearly wanted me to respond. The brief silence gave me some space to frame my reply: 'What does "psychoanalyst" mean to you?'

I had not answered her question, but I appeared to have understood the significance of it, because Hannah came straight back at me, quite forcibly, 'Well, one of those men who see sex in everything – you know, Freud and all that. I've had enough of that sort of thing.' She paused, and then said more wistfully, 'I hoped I'd be able to see a woman.' A suggestion of sadness crossed her face before she returned to a look of agitation.

'You hoped you'd be able to talk to a woman,' I said gently, 'and you find yourself talking to a man. And you're afraid I will only be interested in sex.' It was a slightly risky comment, but I hoped that it was ambiguous enough not to be taken as too rapid an introduction of the significance of the relationship between us (rather than the significance of sex), which would form the basis of any future counselling.

'So you are a psychoanalyst?', Hannah replied, but this time with a hint of a smile. Perhaps she had caught the ambiguity, but it seemed more likely that her smile indicated some relief that I had grasped the nettle of a central issue. I hoped I had handled it gently, neither pretending that my being a man was not of some significance, nor showing too obvious an interest in an area of her life which she had already made clear was in some way threatening to her.

'No, I'm a counsellor. But I *am* interested in what worries you about psychoanalysis . . .'

THE DEVELOPMENT OF PSYCHODYNAMIC THEORY AND PRACTICE

Hannah's initial question suggests similar concerns and confusions about the relationship between counselling and psychoanalysis which appear in some clients and in the general population. We will return to this first session in the next chapter. For the moment Hannah has raised an issue which provides a useful introduction to psychodynamic counselling in action.

Hannah's concern is one which is shared by some counsellors, who are suspicious of anything that smacks of Freud. There is a certain irony in such antipathy. It is, of course, over 100 years since Freud first began to develop his theories and techniques, and since that time nearly every therapeutic method (other than cognitive-behavioural therapy) has evolved from or in reaction to his work. There has been an evolution of therapy and counselling from psychoanalysis, which Hannah would have no reason to know. This development has sometimes led to methods and philosophies which seem quite unrelated to Freud's practice, and which even dismiss his ideas as unhelpful or irrelevant. Some of the models have developed his ideas, others have dismissed controversial aspects of his theories, while others have pioneered apparently new methods.

Of course, Freudian theory and practice have evolved too. Given Hannah's suspicion and her distress, it was inappropriate to explain this to her, or to point out what enormous influence psychoanalysis has had on modern Western thought and popular culture. Hannah's picture of Freud was a one-sided, almost stereotypical one. She did not appear to know (why should she?) that, for example, during his own lifetime he extended his thinking beyond sexuality to look at the problem of death and aggression. (For a straightforward introduction to Freud's life, work in theory

2

and practice as well the influence of his ideas, see Jacobs, 1992.) Since his death in 1939 there has been both considerable reinterpretation of Freud's original models of personality and much greater understanding of the earlier years of life. Indeed, had all this not been so, Freudian therapy could easily have become a psychological backwater.

Hannah raised the question of the emphasis which Freud put on sex. Such questions were raised right at the start of Freud's career, by some of his medical colleagues. At that time it may have been right to resist their own embarrassed sensibilities, and doggedly assert the importance of sexuality as one of the causes of personal neurosis. However, fighting such opposition at that stage made it difficult for Freud to accept the later refinements urged on him by some of his own circle. Jung and Adler, for instance, questioned whether there might not be other factors in the causation of neurosis than sexual tensions; but they were met with such opposition to their own emphases that each was compelled to break away from mainstream psychoanalysis. Jung's work developed as 'analytic psychology' and has been very influential (see particularly Samuels, 1985 for a comprehensive account of the different schools of Jungian theory and practice). Adler is less well known, although some of his ideas find representation in a developed form in therapists such as Karen Horney (Rubins, 1978) and Erich Fromm (see, for example, 1959, 1967); in Britain, Adlerian counselling is not as well known as Adlerian individual psychology is in the United States (for an example of Adlerian counselling in practice, see Miller's chapter in Walker, 1995).

Lists of famous analytic writers are scarcely important, although the reader may wish to place some of the better known ones in relation to each other. Horney and Fromm are amongst the Neo-Freudians, who nearly all left the more orthodox Freudian position on emigrating in the 1930s from Europe to America. Other analysts remained within the mainstream of psychoanalysis. The reader may well have come across a number of the following leading figures: for example, Freud's daughter Anna (Freud, A., 1968, 1973), and Erikson (1965), each representing different forms of what is called ego-psychology; Melanie Klein (Segal, 1992) and Bion (Symington and Symington, 1996) as perhaps the leading Kleinians; Kohut (1971, 1977) and Kernberg (1975), who have developed particular work with the narcissistic personality; Winnicott (1964; Jacobs, 1995), Fairbairn (Sutherland, 1989) and Guntrip (1961, 1971), who are representative of the more independent school in Britain. Others such as Bowlby (1979; Holmes, 1993), Rycroft (1985), Lomas (1973, 1987) or Laing (1965; Kotowicz, 1997) have struck out on their own, and are often critical of certain aspects of psychoanalysis, yet at the same time valuing what they consider to be its strongest points. All these, and many others, have made vital contributions to the development of psychodynamic theory, sometimes building on Freud's later ideas, sometimes restructuring whole sections of the psychological map. Psychodynamic thought, including psychoanalysis itself, is certainly not a monolithic system.

A detailed description of the different theoretical formulations about the development and structure of the personality found in psychodynamic literature could easily become confusing in this context, although there are valuable texts which will take the interested reader further into psychoanalytic and psychodynamic theory and practice (Gomez, 1996; Greenberg and Mitchell, 1983; Klein, 1987; Kohon, 1986; Rayner, 1990). Much modern psychoanalytic theory is called 'object relations theory'. Fortunately the technical aspects of the psychodynamic practice, particularly as applied to psychodynamic counselling, are similar enough to be encompassed within the single description in this book. Past disputes between leading psychodynamic therapists may have resulted in splits into various schools of thought, but these have been replaced in our own time with a certain degree of rapprochement and mutual learning, so that whatever the particular orientation of a psychodynamic counsellor (Freudian, Kleinian, Jungian, Object Relations), there is a fairly common base, from which (at least in this author's view) each practitioner gradually develops his or her own style, informed by a theoretical base, but refined in response to the types of client and setting in which each person works, as well as the personal development of thinking that comes with experience.

Psychoanalysis encompasses a therapeutic technique, and a theoretical model of the human personality. To describe psychodynamic counselling in action I concentrate on how a psychodynamic counsellor approaches the therapeutic task. I have elsewhere demonstrated the way in which theories of personality are used in the practice of psychodynamic counselling and therapy (Jacobs, 1998). Even though I do not dwell on those aspects in this book, as I think they constitute the next stage of learning to practise the psychodynamic approach, it is necessary for a psychodynamic counsellor to know about personal development (distinct from developmental psychology inasmuch as it concentrates upon emotional and inter-personal issues), particularly as described in the models developed variously by analysts such as Sigmund and Anna Freud, Klein, Winnicott, and Erikson from the psychoanalytic perspective, and Jung and various post-Jungians from that of analytical psychology (Samuels, 1985).

My own position is closer to an independent post-Freudian line than to either of the other principal psychodynamic therapies stemming from Jung or Klein, even though I value many of the insights these and other major writers provide for the possibility of deeper understanding of myself and others. Counsellors who style themselves Jungian and Kleinian may sometimes use concepts and terms which differ from Freudian or post-Freudian ideas; in the examples in this book I may occasionally include a psychodynamic formulation with which a Jungian or Kleinian counsellor would disagree. Similarly, symbols in dreams and fantasies can be interpreted in distinctive ways by different schools. However, it needs to be remembered that some of the differences evident in psychodynamic schools are questions of emphasis, or may even be semantic, so that the same experience can be interpreted in different theoretical terms.

Generally, such technical discussions are best reserved for the training setting, for supervision and for case-work discussion, related constantly to practice and to what the client presents. In speaking with the client, we need to use words and descriptions which the individual person can comprehend. A counsellor always has to translate theories into a language which is understood by the client (and which is understood too by the counsellor!), illustrated with evidence that the client has introduced or referred to in the counselling session.

I have already begun to use some technical terms myself. It is important to explain some of the common underlying terms and principles which typify psychodynamic work before considering in more detail, in subsequent chapters, the ways in which these principles are seen in action.

SOME BASIC TERMS: PSYCHODYNAMIC

Given the different theories that have developed from and within psychoanalysis, the word 'psychodynamic' is a useful one since it encompasses the different schools mentioned above. The word 'psychodynamic' links psychotherapy and counselling with psychoanalysis, although the latter has largely come to mean long-term psychotherapy, twice or three times a week. 'Psychodynamic' is a term which is used in the development of ideas and practice of many who have no wish to call themselves Freudian, whatever significance they are willing to attribute to some of his work. It is noticeable, for example, that the psychodynamic approach forms a major part of the thinking and practice of many counsellors and therapists who call themselves 'integrative'. Close demarcations of territory are less in evidence than once they were, except perhaps in certain psychoanalytic circles. Since I myself do not like to be associated with some of the preciousness and rigidity of some psychoanalytic politics, I prefer to use the term 'psychodynamic' as not so historically tainted as the term 'psychoanalytic'. Nevertheless, like others who are critical of aspects of psychoanalysis, I too draw deeply upon the imaginative and thoughtful work and experience of many extremely talented analysts, whose writing is a treasury of insight.

The term 'psychodynamic' clearly needs some explanation. 'Psyche', the root word from which psychology, psychotherapy, psychodynamic, etc. are built, has often been translated in English texts as 'mind' (see Bettelheim, 1983 for many examples of mistranslation of Freud's work). Such a translation carries connotations of intellectual processes alone, whereas 'psyche' includes emotions and feelings. A secular age is not happy with notions of the soul, although some such word as 'spirit' begins to get closer to what psyche means. Psyche, especially as used in psychodynamic literature, means something of all three aspects: thought, feeling, and the spirit of a person. I cannot here discuss the complex ideas there are on the relationship between body, mind, and spirit; nor do I know whether these three constitute the whole person; or even whether there is one Self, or many selves – parts of the psyche, or aspects of the person. It is sufficient to point out that if we think about ourselves, we know there is more to us than mind, more than thought and intellect. Emotions or feelings are an equally important feature, influencing and influenced by interaction with body and mind.

'Psychodynamic' refers to the way in which the psyche (as mind/emotions/spirit/self) is seen as active, and not static. This does not simply mean being active in the sense that thinking and feeling are personal activities; nor does it simply mean forces within the psyche which actively seek expression or satisfaction. The weakness of such terms as 'instincts' or 'drives', which were a major part of Freud's theory (Jacobs, 1992: 39–42), is that they describe activity but do not appear to give sufficient weight to the relationships between people, or to the dynamic between them.

What particularly distinguishes the term 'psychodynamic' is that the activity of the psyche is not confined to relating to people, or to objects outside of the self (there are few who would contend that). Activity also takes place within the psyche, in relation to itself. 'To itself' is not a very accurate phrase, because the psyche, or the personality, seems to consist of a number of 'selves'. This becomes clearer if we consider some very common expressions which we find in everyday speech.

'I don't feel myself today.' Here the speaker presupposes that there is a self which is more normally him than the one he is currently experiencing. Notice also that in this phrase the speaker refers to himself as both the subject of the phrase ('I') and the object ('myself'). This sense of being more than one person appears in other phrases. 'I don't like that side of myself.' Here the speaker refers to a definite part of herself, but a part which she would rather do without. 'It just came over me, and I felt so cross with myself.' Here the speaker refers to three aspects of himself: (a) 'it', as if there were something inside which took over for a while – this is what Freud meant by the Id or, more accurately translated, the It; (b) 'me', which seems more like a central part of the self which got temporarily thrown off-centre, and which may even be blamed for allowing this to happen in the 'myself' at the end of the sentence; (c) 'I', which here seems not to be a central 'I', but more like a critical, even hostile, part of the self.

To analyse such phrases in this way may appear unduly complicated, but such analysis reveals a description of internal relationships, within a person, which do not have to be connected with feelings towards anyone else, and do not rely on an external person for their promptings. We can just as easily love, hate, or fear parts of ourselves as we can other people. There is a dynamic going on within the psyche, as well as between us and other people.

These parts of the self are described in different ways in psychodynamic literature. Such descriptions are attempts to make sense of the phenomena, although the diversity of terms used, even in the psychoanalytic tradition, does not always lead to clarity in the mind of the reader. Freud used the terms Id, Ego and Super-ego to illustrate his 'map' of the internal relations within the psyche (Jacobs, 1992: 57–60). Jung used rather more graphic terms, including the persona, the shadow, anima and animus, painting a quite distinct picture of the different aspects that go to make up the whole person or the Self (Fordham, F., 1953; Samuels, 1985). Winnicott described the True Self and the False Self (1965: 140–52). Melanie Klein developed the idea of 'internal objects' (Segal, 1992: 43–4). Fairbairn (1994) used terms which he preferred to the 'id', and he modified the concept the 'super-ego', since he did not perceive personality structure in the same way as Freud. Although Transactional Analysis is quite distinct from other psychodynamic theories, it too has its own tripartite description: Parent, Adult and Child (Stewart, 1989). These ego-states do not simply describe the Parent–Child relationship, for example, between two people, but can also be applied to an internal state – 'your (internal) Parent is getting at your (internal) Child'.

These internal aspects (or 'objects', as they are sometimes called in psychodynamic literature) of the psyche are formed over the long years of a child's development, as counterparts of external relationships which predominate in early childhood, principally those with mother and father. These aspects are more than pictures in the memory, but are as alive and as real within as once they were without. There is stronger emphasis given to innate factors and predisposition in the Kleinian school; but all psychodynamic theories pay equal attention to the importance of the child's early environment, as promoting the foundation of later personality strengths or areas of vulnerability. Hence the importance that a psychodynamic counsellor attaches to experiences and feelings from the client's past.

The extent to which these 'dynamics' take place within the psyche is underlined by the way in which these internal objects are not modelled on external relationships alone. They are also formed from the particular way in which a child 'sees' others. Thus a psychodynamic approach also includes serious attention to the powerful effect of fantasies. A young child 'thinks' in an uninformed way, less able than an adult to check perceptions against reality. Thus a significant aspect of psychological development comes not simply from the way a mother and father relate to their child, but also from the way in which a child perceives and 'pictures' mother and father. Although these early perceptions and rudimentary understandings are gradually modified by the experience of a wider reality, they are never totally lost. So adults also have occasion to view the world, or particular persons, or even themselves, through the eyes of the child within them. This is especially true at times of stress, when they can be driven back (or to use a psychodynamic term: they 'regress') to more primitive ('infantile', in a non-pejorative sense) ways of thinking, feeling and behaving.

All of these factors contribute to the dynamic forces or activities within the psyche, and to the internal relationships between different parts of the self. The objects of a child's feelings or fantasy are therefore both external, the parents as they actually are, and internal, the parents as they are experienced, particularly at times of stress. The images formed in the child's psyche are not simply pictures of the parents, but become internalised objects, indistinguishable parts of the self, yet with an apparent life of their own. So, to return to the simple phrase used earlier, 'I felt so cross with myself': the 'I' in this sense owes something to my parents when they were actually cross with me; something to the fantasy that my parents would be cross with me if they knew what I was doing; something to the frustration that might have led to me also being cross with them; and something to this series of images amalgamating into a punitive part of myself, called the 'super-ego' by Freudians, or more popularly known as 'conscience'.

Such a lengthy excursion into the meaning of 'psychodynamic' may seem a long way from early Freudian ideas of the child as a bundle of mainly sexual instincts, waiting to be satisfied. Like many others, Hannah (in the example with which this chapter started) had a dated view of psychoanalysis. Her inaccurate perception may have been partly due to her fantasy as well as her ignorance. Psychoanalysis and other psychodynamic approaches no longer suggest a psyche in which the dominant primitive part hungrily waits to be fed, is bursting to defecate, or longs to have sexual release. Psychodynamic functioning is both more complex and more complete than that. It includes the powerful feelings in relationships, both between people (parent and child, husband and wife, within a family or a group) and between the different aspects of a person's psyche. The term 'relationship' is more significant than might be apparent from reading early Freudian literature, and far more important to modern psychodynamic theory than Freud's instinct theory. The love and the hate between a parent and a child, and within each of them, are just as significant as orality, anality and sexuality – the stages of the original Freudian developmental scheme (Freud, 1905).

Hence the appeal of a different term in post-Freudian theory known as Object Relations theory, which expresses more clearly the way in which psychodynamic thinking has developed, although the word 'object' may at first seem impersonal. An approximate synonym for 'Object Relations' is 'Personal Relationships'. The reason why the latter, more readily understandable phrase is not used is because psychodynamic theory also attaches significance to the *object* of a person's feelings or desires, which may be non-human (as Winnicott used the term 'transitional object', 1958: 229–42), or part of a person (the breast, for example, in the earliest mother–baby relationship). Apart from relationships to whole persons, the psychodynamic therapist and counsellor is therefore concerned to understand the relationships the client has to her or his own internal objects (the internalised aspects of the personality referred to above); to what are known as 'part-objects' (parts of the body, as well as persons who are perceived only partially, and not as a whole); and to non-human objects (such as a child's security blanket as in some sense 're-presenting' the nurturing, but temporarily absent, parent).

These ideas may appear complicated, but if I have conveyed nothing else, I trust I have communicated a sense of the psyche as including limitless activity, constantly humming with life, whatever the more obvious state of mind that is apparent on the surface. Although we are more conscious of the ceaseless activity at particular times of stress and agitation, this activity is also experienced quite markedly in dreams, when even the most staid conscious mind often gives way to the frenetic adventures of the unconscious psyche. Modern psychodynamic theory understands the different figures in dreams as representing various aspects of the self. Apart from dreams and other fantasies which a client may relate, the psychodynamic counsellor is also alive to the various indicators of psychodynamic activity in the way the client talks about situations past and present and, as we shall see, in the counselling relationship itself.

THE UNCONSCIOUS

This is another term requiring explanation, because it is frequently surrounded by myth and mystification. Freud distinguished between mental activity which is conscious (that is, what we are currently thinking and feeling), that which is not conscious but easily becomes so, such as a memory of a fact, a feeling or an event (Freud called this the 'preconscious') and 'mental processes or mental material which have no easy access to consciousness, but which must be inferred, discovered and translated into conscious form' (Freud, 1940: 20); it was for this category that Freud reserved the name 'the unconscious' (Jacobs, 1992: 31–3).

The importance of the unconscious for Freud and for those who followed him makes it one of the principal hypotheses of psychodynamic work. The term is not original, because it was a concept current in some of the literature and philosophy of his day. Perhaps Freud gave more substance to the term, through his determination to show the significance of unconscious material. It was in fact hypnosis which first alerted Freud to the influence of the unconscious, since he found that certain memories seemed accessible only to this particular form of suggestion. Hypnosis, long since abandoned in psychodynamic practice, certainly demonstrates the way in which mind and body can be influenced both during and even some time after the hypnotic experience.

One of the original aims of psychoanalysis was, as it still is in all psychodynamic work, to make the unconscious conscious; and in doing so, to help a person to act with more conscious control and awareness than unconscious reactions permit: 'where id was, there shall ego be', as Freud put it. In fact, this is a somewhat limited definition of the aim of psychotherapy and counselling. His later formula, put in more straightforward terms, suggests that successful psychotherapy and counselling enables a person to balance the often conflicting demands of basic psychological (and some physiological) needs; the demands of conscience (which is not always 'bad'); and the demands of the external reality of the situation: 'an action by the ego is as it should be if it satisfies simultaneously the demands of the id, of the super-ego and of reality' (Freud, 1940: 377–8).

The 'unconscious' is, by definition, not conscious. It is therefore unknowable. This makes it a difficult concept to picture, since what was unconscious is only seen when it is no longer unconscious! Although some memories readily come to mind (and show the value of the distinctive term 'preconscious'), others are hidden so deep that, should they be recalled, the experience has the quality of surprise, even novelty, about it – 'I had *completely* forgotten that', as if the event was being experienced almost (though not quite) for the first time. Furthermore, although some people may remember events and situations quite accurately, they are not always conscious of the feelings which they then experienced; as if those feelings were not allowed to surface at the time, but were submerged, or 'repressed' – to use a psychodynamic term. Repression frequently leads to feelings and thoughts being denied in the present as well as in the past. For instance, as Hannah was later to recall, when they were evicted from their home, she suppressed her grief at leaving, so as not to upset her grandfather. Those feelings of grief were set to one side. What she was unconscious of at that time, and right up to a certain point in her counselling, was how angry she felt with her grandfather's responsibility for their eviction. When she caught a glimpse of that anger, she said, 'I never realised that's how I felt.' Her grief was *suppressed* – unexpressed but not forgotten; her anger was *repressed*, not only unexpressed but also forgotten.

There is yet another sense in which the 'unconscious' can be understood. If I point out to someone how they are reacting, they may not realise it until I make the observation. They are not conscious of what they are doing, or saying. They may not, of course, acknowledge something so obvious to others; they remain unconscious (unknowing, unseeing) of themselves.

So there is no need to mystify the term 'unconscious'. It is a useful image with which to describe certain phenomena, and even to conceptualise the dynamics of the psyche, in which some feelings, certain ideas and even whole experiences appear to be pushed into hiding, because they are too threatening or too painful for the conscious self to acknowledge or experience at the time.

Many of the psychodynamic terms can be more fully understood and appreciated if they can be seen more as metaphors than as statements to be taken literally. The 'unconscious' is one of those metaphors, which attempts to describe the indescribable, one of several images which psychodynamic thought makes considerable use of, in its attempt to make sense of experience. Whether or not the unconscious exists as a separate entity is a somewhat fruitless argument. Like many other concepts in psychodynamic theory, it is a useful notion to have, in order to possess a type of therapeutic map.

Freud drew two different diagrams, in his various attempts to illustrate the workings of the conscious and unconscious, and of the id, ego and super-ego. He knew they were of limited value, serving more as crude pictures of the relationship between conscious and unconscious functions within the psyche. They describe nonetheless the type of psychological experience to which I alluded above: the sense of there being more than one person within the self; the feeling that there is 'a place' in the mind, to which unpleasant or unacceptable memories, feelings and fantasies are banished; or that the psyche sometimes seems a kind of 'prison' from which these painful feelings and memories crave release. It is not unusual to feel that we sometimes act less freely than we wish, as if influenced by some other aspect deep within the self.

These feelings about ourselves may help us to unpack what Freud and his followers mean by the term 'the unconscious' and the structure of the personality. Freud's translators made a serious mistake when they gave many of his more straightforward terms a scientific twist. As Bettelheim (1983) points out, ego, id and super-ego should have been translated 'I', 'It' and 'Over-I' – words which are both more expressive of personal feeling, and less scientifically pretentious. Psychodynamic thought can only be understood if it recognised that its images and metaphors are ways of attempting to codify experiences and aspects of the personality. As I have already indicated above, counsellors should always communicate with their clients using words and images that their clients understand and recognise as relevant to their personal situation. In the end, theory can be used only as long as it makes sense of clients' experience, and when it fits what clients describe.

DIFFERENT LAYERS OF UNDERSTANDING

Many books have been written in which these and other psychodynamic concepts are discussed, and in which attempts are made to structure a psychodynamic understanding of personal development and of the internal relationships within the psyche. It needs to be stressed that the raw material from which such theories are formed normally comes out of the practice of psychotherapy and counselling; indeed some psychologists and other critics observe that the weakness of psychoanalytic theories is that they are based upon individual case-work, and not on extensive research using greater numbers of people.

For the psychodynamic counsellor in action theories provide signposts. They act as rough maps which serve as guides through the often bewildering territory into which the counsellor is led. The primary purpose in psychodynamic counselling is to help clients to make sense of current situations; of feelings and thoughts evoked by those situations; of memories associated with their present experience, some of which spring readily to mind, others of which may rise to consciousness as the counselling develops; and of the images that appear in fantasies and dreams. Often present feelings and fantasies are linked to the past, by the client as much as by the counsellor, and memories of events, of relationships, of feelings and fantasies also form part of the content of the session. From this wealth of material a psychodynamic counsellor attempts to form a picture, representing not just the way in which the client relates, or wishes to relate to others, but also the way the client relates to her- or himself. This may be linked to ways in which the client describes past relationships, and often will be linked to the way the client and counsellor themselves relate. Inevitably, counselling, sometimes shorn of the luxury of time which longer-term therapy permits, only catches glimpses of the whole, and must often remain content with working on a segment of the complete picture. Nevertheless all the elements are there, if sometimes only in miniature.

One such glimpse of the way in which a segment gives a hint of a more complete picture is seen in the question which Hannah asked in the opening example. It shows the different levels at which a phrase might be understood. She apparently wanted a purely factual piece of information, but clearly had feelings which gave the question more than intellectual significance. She did not simply have a somewhat narrow view of psychoanalysis, which could be explained as straightforward and understandable ignorance. She was also concerned lest psychoanalysis meant that sex was going to be the main focus between herself and me. It was possible that she was not simply unsure of talking about the subject of sex: she might also be afraid, because she was a woman and I (the counsellor) was a man, that the gender relationship could become an issue between us, in terms of the feelings which might be aroused in her or in me towards each other. From what she said it seemed as if sex had been an issue, of which she had 'had enough', sometime in the past, even before seeing me. Even in those opening words there were hints that she was presenting me with an important aspect of her current problems, whatever they might be. She was also warning me that this was a subject which she was not readily going to talk about.

It is this many-layered way of understanding the client, and of helping the client to understand her- or himself, which forms the core of psycho-dynamic counselling. Many of those layers were already present, if only as possibilities, in the opening moments of the first session with Hannah. Somewhere and sometime in the past, for instance, there might have been difficulties which could be linked to her present anxiety about coming to see me – problems perhaps about sex and/or about close relationships with men. The possible significance of her words led me naturally into some questions which indicated my psychodynamic interest in what she meant, and into her previous experience and history. What has happened in Hannah's past? What has she experienced, both in reality and in her perception of reality? What has she felt in the past? These were all perti-nent questions as I started counselling with Hannah, even though at this stage I had no idea of whether or not such history would turn out to be relevant, or how it might relate to her present problems.

However much of a client's personal history emerges, the psychody-namic approach is distinct from other models of counselling, in that the counsellor remains aware of the developmental issues described in psy-chodynamic theory, using these ideas to try to throw light on what a client says, and on the way a client reacts to the counsellor – even though it is not always possible in counselling to make definite links between the past and the present. In this book, which is concerned more with counselling in action than with psychodynamic theories of personal development, I will not attempt to expand upon psychodynamic models of personal development. I have written much more fully on this elsewhere (Jacobs, 1998), where I demonstrate the richness with which a client's past experi-ence can inform present situations. I also hope, within the two case-histories that run throughout this book, to provide examples of the significance of personal history for the client and the counsellor, and to illustrate the interaction of the past and present. Psychodynamic counselling, wherever possible, constantly moves between these different levels, each one illustrating the others.

This link between past and present can as yet only be half-perceived in what Hannah said. It was too soon to be able to say whether the difficulty she had already expressed, about seeing a male counsellor, was also present in her current relationships with other men apart from myself. At this early stage I knew nothing more about her. I would, however, hazard a guess that this was so, while remaining ready to be proved wrong. Neither did I know at that stage whether her concern about sex was based upon actual experience, or upon experiences which might, with some justification, have been interpreted as threatening in her thoughts and fantasies about me; or whether the threat was largely a fantasy with no obvious antecedents in reality. What I did know was that Hannah, in asking whether I was a psychoanalyst, was also telling me some important information about herself, which time might help me to fathom.

THE COUNSELLING RELATIONSHIP AND TRANSFERENCE

There are links between the external and internal 'worlds' of the client, that is between relationships to others and the internal relationships within the psyche. There are links between past and present experience. There are, furthermore, links between what is talked about as occurring outside the counselling session, and what takes place in the relationship between counsellor and client. The parallel is two-way, and psychodynamic counselling concurs with many other counselling methods in that in the immediacy of the counselling situation there are clues to, and sometimes obvious signs of, the way the client relates and responds to others outside the counselling room. Hannah demonstrated this when she talked about not really wanting to see a man, hinting at the possibility, which had yet to be confirmed, that she might find difficulty relating openly or trustingly to other men as well.

The relationship between the counsellor and the client is indeed reckoned to be a crucial aspect in nearly every school of counselling, and psychodynamic counselling is no exception. The counselling relationship needs to be more than a good working relationship, and it requires particular qualities in the counsellor if the right conditions are to be present in which the client can develop as a person. The immediacy of that relationship frequently demonstrates how the client might feel in other situations, or how others might experience the client. None of this is any the less relevant to the psychodynamic counsellor. Perhaps what distinguishes the psychodynamic approach from others is the way in which the relationship can be understood – what is known as 'the transference'.

I return to a fuller explanation of transference in Chapter 6. Briefly, transference is the repetition by the client of former, often child-like, patterns of relating to significant people, such as parents, but now seen in relation to the counsellor. Use of the transference makes it one of the most distinct features of psychodynamic theory and practice. As I explain later, transference is not a phenomenon that happens only in counselling. Transference phenomena occur in every human relationship. In psychodynamic therapy and counselling particular attention is paid to the transference, by attempting to show how it influences the relationship between client and therapist. There are counsellors of other persuasions who do not attach any value to the concept of transference; but the psychodynamic counsellor, even looking at other types of therapy, can often detect the presence of transference, sometimes helping, sometimes hindering, the client's progress.

For instance, counsellors rightly stress the necessity of unconditional regard – the ability to accept others, whatever they say or do, without preconditions. Viewed psychodynamically, this quality in the counsellor represents for the client the transferring on to the counselling relationship of all that is good in the parent–child relationship. The psychodynamic counsellor would therefore expect such unconditional regard to encourage what is known as a positive transference relationship between counsellor and client. The counsellor becomes, for the client, a transference figure with whom the client has the opportunity to re-live the type of parent–child relationship he or she might have wished for, or even to some extent had. Where the parents of the client conveyed some of the acceptance and trust he or she also feels in their counsellor, this transference presents little problem, and probably calls for little comment. If, however, the client's parenting has left the client distrustful and suspicious of others, including parental figures such as those in helping professions, the counsellor can understand any reticence the client shows towards her or himself: the client appears to be transferring the original negative experience of the parent–child relationship on to the counselling relationship, unable to accept the unconditional regard which the counsellor is trying to convey.

There are important differences between that type of counselling which attempts to provide a positive corrective experience for the client through the attitudes of the counsellor, and the more deliberate use of the trans-ference. (I will be examining Clarkson's (1995) useful identification of the developmentally needed relationship in Chapter 6.) One difference is that a psychodynamic counsellor can bring the presence of transference feel-ings in the client out into the open, and work with the client to understand them. I did this with Hannah in a subtle way when I suggested to her that she was afraid that, like Freud, I would be interested only in sex. I felt that she had a perception of Freud which she had transferred on to psycho-analysis as a whole, and on to me as a counsellor in particular. It was far too early for me to want to look for an explanation of this transference and of her anxiety, but mentally I noted the possibility that she might be transferring on to Freud at a distance, and on to me closer to, some past experience of feeling a man's salacious sexual interest in her. The reader will have to wait, as I myself did, to see whether there were indeed any grounds for such an hypothesis.

NEGATIVE TRANSFERENCE AND THE REPETITION OF FAILURE

There is another important emphasis in the psychodynamic use of the transference, which makes the psychodynamic view of the role of the counsellor quite different from many other counselling methods. This is the recognition of the therapeutic value of the negative aspects of the counsellor–client relationship. Many counselling approaches encourage the growth of the client through the positive regard and other core con-ditions demonstrated by the counsellor with the client (Mearns and Thorne, 1988). In doing so, understood in psychodynamic terms, such counsellors attempt to recreate conditions which might have been absent or lacking in the client's past experience. Psychodynamic counselling does not in any way undervalue these basic aspects of the counselling rela-tionship. At the same time, the psychodynamic approach also takes into account the impossibility of the counsellor ever being able to become the type of good and loving parent whom the client might have wished for. The counsellor is also a person who inevitably *repeats* the parental failures and short-comings with the client. 'He can never make up to clients for what they have suffered in the past, but what he can do is to repeat the fail-ure to love them enough . . . and then share with them and help them work through their feelings about his failure' (Winnicott, quoted in Malan, 1979: 141).

17

Counselling can at times involve as much disappointment for the client as it does satisfaction. The counsellor cannot, for instance, be present for the client as much as he or she might hope, nor does the counsellor provide the clear guidance and advice which the client might expect. The counsellor cannot be a friend or an intimate partner in the way that a client might sometimes wish. In these and so many other ways, the counsellor, simply by acting as a counsellor should, forces the client to re-live negative experiences which go on influencing the present, including the frustration that accompanied past experiences, and which may still accompany present relationships. While some clients' problems are caused by obvious, deliberate, and traumatic maltreatment on the part of parents, all too often the 'failure' of parenting occurs in what is *not* done as much as by what is done. This includes the unavoidable failure of the parent to be the ideal figure whom the child somewhat unrealistically wished for, an internalised parent figure who goes on being mourned, or even punished, in the child's inner world. Psychodynamic theory, we remember, takes account of the power of fantasy, as much as the power of fact, to distort perceptions and relationships.

There is a small example of this failure on the part of the counsellor in the opening moments with Hannah. She had wanted a woman for her counsellor. I drew attention to the fact that she found herself talking to a man, wondering whether she might take that up, either by expressing her negative feelings about me being a man, or alternatively by saying what talking to a woman would have meant for her. Again, we have to wait and see whether this disappointment meant more to Hannah than she had so far voiced and, if so, what that disappointment signified.

One way in which the counsellor will appear to fail many clients is through the ending of sessions and the conclusion of counselling itself. That failure is felt in a variety of ways: some clients feel let down through not having achieved as much as they had initially hoped for; others feel rejected by the counsellor; some feel angry, others sad, a few even glad to get away. I look at endings in Chapter 7, but here draw attention to a further central feature of psychodynamic therapy and counselling, which is the emphasis on working with loss, including loss of the counsellor. Although the brevity of some counselling contracts does not permit the development of much dependency on the part of the client, even short-term counselling holds out considerable hope to the new client. Whether its duration is long or short, counselling involves sessions which last for less than an hour, breaks at holiday time, occasional alterations because of illness or other exigencies, and a comparatively short contract for the number of sessions. These breaks and endings repeat the limitations which everyone experiences throughout life, but which were felt more acutely in early childhood; they therefore provide opportunities for clients to work through early frustrations and losses in the 'here-and-now' – in the relationship between client and counsellor.

MAKING ACTIVE USE OF RESISTANCE

Psychodynamic technique therefore differs from some other schools of therapy (except where they too draw upon psychodynamic concepts) in the deliberate, although not necessarily overt, use of the transference relationship alongside the actual relationship between counsellor and client. I illustrate how this can be used in subsequent chapters. Another major focus in psychodynamic therapy and counselling is understanding and working with resistance. Resistance, which takes different forms, describes those times when clients cannot or will not talk freely, or are unable to acknowledge thoughts and feelings, because they are afraid of what will emerge, and are concerned about their or the counsellor's reaction. Even though a counsellor often has less time available for a client than a psychotherapist can offer, he or she cannot hurry the process. Clients have to work at their own pace, as all sensitive counselling approaches recognise. This does not prevent the counsellor from acknowledging the resistance which clients show, both to insight into themselves, and also to cognitive or behavioural change. Of course clients want to change, or they wish things could change, otherwise they would not have sought help in the first instance. At the same time they are frightened of what they may learn in the process, or what may happen if they alter ways of being, relating or acting.

Hannah showed a hint of a possible resistance when she mentioned having had 'enough of that sort of thing', with reference to sex. She was making it clear that I might get metaphorically slapped down if I explored that particular subject. What distinguishes the psychodynamic approach is the recognition that resistance has to be handled by understanding the *reasons* for such defensiveness. The counsellor is as interested in understanding the defence, as in anything that the client might be defending against. Only the client can withdraw the resistance, although a skilful and sensitive helper tries to interpret (and help the client understand) the reasons for resistance. The counsellor remains aware that resistance renders the results of short-term work less penetrating than might be the case in longer psychotherapy. I discuss this issue further in Chapter 5.

A 'RULE' FOR THE COUNSELLOR AND A 'RULE' FOR THE CLIENT

Nearly all counsellors encourage their clients to express their own agenda and to explore their feelings, thoughts and fantasies, by deliberately holding back at points when in normal social conversation they would usually say more. Such holding back is known in psychodynamic work as the 'rule of abstinence'. It does not mean total silence, or being an impersonal blank screen, but it does involve being careful not to intrude upon what the client is trying to reach. To some extent this attitude on the part of the counsellor or therapist complements, and yet contrasts with, another 'rule': that the client should express 'everything that comes into his head' (Freud, 1940: 407). Freud put it this way, we gather, to his patients:

> You will notice that as you relate things various thoughts will occur to you which you would like to put aside on the grounds of certain criticisms or objections. You will be tempted to say to yourself that this or that is irrelevant here, or is quite unimportant, or nonsensical, so that there is no need to say it. You must never give in to these criticisms, but say it in spite of them . . . (Freud, 1913: 134–5)

Most counsellors prefer to encourage this freedom of expression without laying it down as a rule (which might only serve to increase a client's anxiety or resistance). The reason for this latter 'fundamental rule' (as Freud called it) and the 'rule of abstinence' is to encourage the client, to put it simply, to 'let things slip out': all that the client says, not just the feelings behind the words, nor just the facts within a situation, but all the apparently insignificant details contain the possibility of providing more understanding of the client's fears and fantasies. Needless to say, the counsellor's abstinence may give rise to negative feelings in the client, who may see in the counsellor's withholding the same failure to provide good enough care, which he or she may have experienced from parents as a child.

There is an early example of the use of this rule of abstinence in the opening of the 'conversation' with Hannah. When she asked me, 'Are you a psychoanalyst?', I did not initially answer her question, as I might in any other conversation. I wanted to know what the term meant to her, in order to have some basis for exploring the fears and fantasies she might have about coming to see me. Her reply furnished some initial possibilities for thinking about her internal world and her past and present relationships.

This deliberate attempt to weave various factors together, including apparently innocuous phrases, in search of a shape to the emerging patterns, probably gives the psychodynamic approach a distinctive position between, on the one hand, those approaches to counselling which stress the client doing the understanding, and, on the other hand, those where the counsellor takes a much more active role.

Whatever rules, whatever techniques, and whatever theories psychodynamic counselling may use, nothing is cast-iron and immutable. The reader will have noticed that I did eventually answer Hannah's question. There are times when rules cease to be helpful, and techniques need to be adapted, just as theories must always be open to adjustment and change. In the example above, I felt both that I wanted to ease unnecessary anxiety, and also that I had gained enough from my initial abstaining from answering her question to be able to tell Hannah that I was not an analyst. Indeed, it was important not to mislead her into thinking that I was other than I am. To abstain further would have laid claim to a false status; and I am not into that.

PSYCHODYNAMIC COUNSELLING AND PSYCHOANALYSIS

In discussing Hannah's question to me about whether I was a psychoanalyst, I hope I have made it clear that psychodynamic counselling is not psychoanalysis, nor is it long-term psychotherapy. Psychodynamic counselling has many resemblances to psychodynamic psychotherapy, and where the contract becomes at all extended the two terms are to some extent interchangeable. There are interesting questions about differences which I have raised, but not resolved, elsewhere (Jacobs, 1994). But there are certain adaptations that have to be made in order to use the psychodynamic approach in counselling.

Contracts are shorter, but actually assume a significance which is not so apparent in long-term therapy, where there may be no definite time limit. I discuss this further in Chapter 4 (see also my chapter in Sills, 1997). Working once a week with a person, rather than several times a week, puts some limits on the type of client who can be seen, although experienced psychodynamic counsellors often see clients who are as damaged as any seen by the majority of psychotherapists. I examine the question of suitable clients in Chapter 3. Aims in counselling are necessarily more limited. Finding a focus for the counsellor's attention, and even for the client's goals, may sometimes be desirable, given the mass of information which some clients produce. There is a sense in which the counsellor has to think more quickly (while at the same time maintaining the right pace for the client) because the opportunities for accurate and helpful interventions are much reduced. Psychodynamic counselling involves condensing the psychoanalytic method; but this can be very taxing, because her or his psychodynamic training cannot help but make the counsellor aware just how complex the human personality is, and just how slow the process of change is. Yet despite the limited objectives of the counsellor, significant shifts in perception do take place and vital insights are achieved, both through the natural wish of the client to progress and through the careful application of the psychodynamic method. The psychodynamic approach, which the counsellor also shows in action in her or his work with the client, is also often adopted by the client in self-analysis, as the process becomes yet another of the internalised relationships in the client's psyche.

Such is the influence of Freudian thought on Western culture that the psychodynamic approach is not as strange as it might appear in cold print. In this chapter the main distinguishing features of psychodynamic counselling, modelled as it is on longer-term psychotherapy, have been introduced. These are: the interrelationship of external and internal worlds, regression under stress, object relations, the unconscious, the significance of the past, and its repetition in the present, the transference relationship between client and counsellor, the value of failure on the part of the therapist, the use of endings, the importance of understanding resistance, and the rule of abstinence. Later chapters show these various features in action.

Although some of these expressions may appear technical, my guess is that counsellors of different theoretical persuasions already use some of these techniques and this understanding, sometimes without knowing their psychoanalytic origins. While it is important that I concentrate upon what is distinctive, I would wish at the same time to affirm that certain basic approaches to counselling, common to different methods, are equally important in psychodynamic work. Indeed, some of these basic techniques and assumptions either owe their origins to, or are at least prefigured in, the development of Freud's own approach to listening, when he moved away from more directive and questioning methods into hearing what his patients were trying to tell him.

There are, of course, significant emphases in different counselling methods, but there is also much which the different approaches share. My description of the psychodynamic approach to counselling in subsequent chapters is bound to include responses and techniques with which other counsellors will concur, as well as features which are more distinct. It is my hope that what is common to various forms of counselling in action will help the reader feel more at ease than Hannah did at our initial meeting; and that anything which turns out to be unique to psychodynamic counselling, and therefore perhaps new to the reader, will help expand the range of possibilities open to the counsellor.

2

THE FIRST SESSION

HANNAH'S REPLY

'But I *am* interested in what worries you about psychoanalysis . . .', I had said.

Hannah thought for a while; the silence felt less tense. She looked across: 'I'm not sure what I'm doing here. I didn't expect this.'

'You didn't expect this,' I repeated.

'No; I've been feeling very low, and I went to my doctor. I thought she'd give me something to take, but she said I should see you. Has she told you about me?'

'What was it you told her?' My question once again moved the initiative back to Hannah.

'I'm not sure I can tell *you*.' She frowned, and looked anxious again.

'Perhaps it's difficult to tell me because I'm a man?'

Hannah nodded, but said nothing. She looked a little sad.

'You wanted to go on seeing your doctor?' I added.

'She hasn't got time, I know. There are a lot more people who deserve more attention than me.' Her eyes had begun to moisten.

'That sounds confusing for you. You're not sure you can speak to me; but part of you wants someone to pay attention to what you're feeling; but you aren't sure whether you've got any value compared to other people . . .'

I spoke slowly, separating out the several conflicting feelings within her. As I spoke, Hannah looked more upset; when I stopped speaking she buried her head in her hands, and began to cry. She bent forward, still on the edge of the chair. She was close enough for me to touch her, and there was indeed within me a feeling that, were this not a counselling setting, comfort might be something I could have offered, since I felt in myself the sadness which she seemed to be experiencing. But I sat absolutely still, remained silent, and wondered at the change that there had been over these opening minutes of the session.

REFERRAL

There is a sense in which counselling starts before a client meets a counsellor, partly because many people first see the counsellor at the suggestion of a third party – in Hannah's case it was her doctor who had referred her to me. We shall continually notice, as the case examples unfold, that nothing is too small for the attention of the psychodynamic counsellor. How Hannah came to me and the manner of the referral were important for a number of reasons. First, any reaction to being 'sent' to someone else needs to be understood, especially if it gets in the way of the development of trust and co-operation between the counsellor and the client. Secondly, the explanation of what counselling is likely to achieve, and therefore the expectations of the client, may be prejudiced by the way in which the referral is made, particularly if it is clumsily or hastily handled. Thirdly, the referral itself sometimes repeats similar circumstances in the client's life experience (as we shall shortly see was the case with Hannah), and so in itself forms part of the raw material which the counsellor uses to understand psychodynamic patterns in the client.

Hannah was referred by her doctor, to whom she had gone expecting a prescription – but instead she was offered a different kind of help. She might have felt some resentment towards her doctor for not acceding to her actual request, but instead sending her off to see a counsellor. If this resentment was felt at all, however, it seemed aimed more in my direction than towards her doctor, whom she perhaps wished to go on seeing. She had already told me that she had hoped to talk to a woman rather than a man, and her doctor had clearly fulfilled that requirement. However, Hannah did not appear conscious of any anger towards her doctor for passing her on. Instead, she explained it by turning some of that anger on herself – she felt she was less deserving of the doctor's attention than the other patients.

It happened that I knew the doctor well, and guessed that she would have handled the referral sensitively – indeed, had she not done so it is doubtful whether Hannah would have made the appointment at all. I realised that the doctor could have referred Hannah to several people, and yet she had chosen to refer her to me, a man, rather than to a woman counsellor. She had not sent me, nor had I asked for, a detailed report on Hannah – many counsellors prefer to make their own assessment of a client rather than have their first impressions coloured by someone else's point of view. My assumption was that her doctor had heard enough of Hannah's story to make the decision that a male counsellor might ultimately be more help to Hannah, even though Hannah would more readily have accepted referral to a woman counsellor. Such decisions are often delicate ones, and sometimes vital to the making of a successful referral, because there are clients who find it impossible to work with one gender or the other. Similar considerations may also attach to any disjunction in ethnic background. The person referring needs to assess whether any such hesitancy could be overcome, because it is probably more helpful for a person to work with the type of person who normally makes them anxious than with someone who appears too comfortable. If Hannah has problems relating to men, then working with a man will arouse more of her feelings, in the here and now, than working with a woman would, where such feelings would always be at one remove. Psychodynamic counselling involves much more than talking about difficulties – it also means trying to face them in the 'here-and-now' of the therapeutic relationship, which often involves transference implications. There is therefore some similarity to a behavioural model of counselling, where there is encouragement to the client to face fears; but in psychodynamic counselling this is not achieved as much by deliberately contrived situations, as might happen in a behavioural desensitisation programme. Rather, the counsellor looks for ways in which problem areas in a client's life naturally arise in the course of the counselling relationship itself.

The doctor had not told Hannah much about my counselling orientation, or, if she had, Hannah was not letting me know it. Hannah implied that she had not quite known what to expect. The referring doctor had done enough to help Hannah make her own appointment to see me, leaving her to take that important initiative; otherwise she had avoided raising any expectations about counselling or about my effectiveness. The doctor had recognised that, apart from discussing with Hannah any immediate doubts she might have which would otherwise prevent her making an appointment, it was best to leave any questions which Hannah had for her to raise with me herself.

Not all referrals are made so well. Some can be made quite dismissively, for example, 'I can't help you any more, you'd better go and see a counsellor'. Some contain hints of a dire diagnosis, for example, 'You really need to see someone who specialises in mental problems'. Some imply magical solutions will be found, for example, 'I suggest you go and see X; he'll soon put you right; he knows everything there is to know about depression'. Some referrals are forced upon the unwilling client, for example, 'Just hang on a minute while I phone through to the counsellor and make an appointment for you to see her'. Some put doubts on the validity of counselling, revealing their prejudice against the value of talking, for example, 'I don't really go on it much myself, but it might be worth seeing a counsellor a few times'. Such scepticism invites the client to expect failure. Some helpers refer quite inappropriately, saying to the counsellor, for example, 'I've got a lovely case for you, as mad as a hatter, I'll send him along; I think you'll find him very interesting'. Some referrers set up a conspiratorial alliance between themselves and the counsellor, for instance, by sending a letter with the client, which the counsellor is expected to open and read in front of the client before the client speaks. Others expect to be kept in touch with the progress of counselling, by asking for informal or formal reports from time to time of the counsellor – of which the client is supposed to know nothing. With such variety of referrals, and of ways of arranging them, the counsellor needs to listen carefully for signs or hints of what coming for counselling means to the client, and of the way in which the referral has been handled.

Prior information from the referrer can sometimes be useful, although many counsellors (of different schools) prefer to reserve such knowledge until after the first session, when they have first had the chance to assess the client from their own perspective. It may be that a referrer's letter confirms what the counsellor has felt; on the other hand, it may present another side of the client which the counsellor has not yet seen. People can present themselves differently to various helpers. Hannah (I learned later) had appeared much more co-operative to her doctor, and more willing to accept the referral, than was evident from the early part of her first session with me. I surmised from that information that Hannah was likely to be more compliant to the wishes of other women – even to the point of suppressing her own feelings about any suggestion she disagreed with or had doubts about; and that she was more suspicious, and even hostile, when it came to her dealings with men.

A SECOND EXAMPLE

Some clients are less suitable for the psychodynamic approach in particular, while there are others who are unlikely to receive much help from any other method of counselling. I look at the criteria of suitability in Chapter 3. Generally speaking, a counsellor, given the choice, will take on clients who appear able to respond to the method which he or she usually practises. So the first session is an opportunity for both counsellor and client to make some kind of assessment of their ability to work together. On the part of the counsellor, this assessment includes whether the client is likely to make good use of the time offered, and whether insight will contribute to behavioural change. On the part of the client, there will often be a feeling, one way or the other, of whether counselling ('just talking about it') offers hope of change. The client will nearly always be considering whether the particular counsellor appears to be someone with whom it is possible to talk and share personal problems, although it has to be said that some clients are so desperate that they appear willing to take a gamble on anyone. In such instances the responsible counsellor might have to draw attention to the unpredictability of the outcome of any counselling, since false promises and exaggerated hopes form a weak basis for the therapeutic partnership. Working with the second client, whom I now introduce, could have started on such a basis had I not been wary of his initial presentation.

The assessment of the suitability of a client starts in the opening moments of the first session. If, in the first few minutes, the client presents what appears to be an almost impossible scenario, which causes the counsellor to doubt whether psychodynamic and/or short-term counselling is appropriate, the session has to be used to assist the client to find the right resources for his particular problem. Sometimes it is not obvious from the first session alone whether the client is suitable or not; but on occasion the counsellor entertains sufficient doubts about the suitability of the psychodynamic approach for a particular client to make him or her more active in investigating particular questions. Such questions are usually aimed at getting information which will enable a more rapid appraisal to be made than the counsellor would normally find necessary. Where there is some doubt the psychodynamic counsellor may work towards a more comprehensive history of the client than would otherwise be the case in a first session. I explain more about history-taking with suitable clients below, and about assessment in the next chapter.

Information which the counsellor seeks might include evidence of the

28

severity and duration of previous disturbances, the original and subsequent onset of particular symptoms, whether the client has been hospitalised or treated by a psychiatrist, or is on any medication from the doctor, whether the client has unsuccessfully sought help elsewhere, or rejected it when it was offered, and suicide risk. Sometimes a client is in fact suitable for a psycho-dynamic approach, but the time available for counselling suggests the need for a particular focus – which again might make the counsellor rather more active in steering the direction of the sessions than was once felt to be the-oretically desirable. Nevertheless psychodynamic counselling is suitable for short-term work, and the reader may wish to follow up particular ways of delivering it through, for example, Malan and Osimo (1992) or Molnos (1995). Alternatively, if the client has the time and there are resources which are available, someone who is not suitable for short-term counselling can be referred for longer-term counselling or psychotherapy.

The second client whom I wish to introduce, Karl, is a case in point. From his opening words, he appeared less immediately suitable for short-term psychodynamic counselling. Karl looked pleased to see me when I met him and took him into my room. He was about fifty, his untidy hair white and thinning on top. He was dressed quite shabbily, with his worn beige overcoat open, his scuffed brown boots needing a polish, and his trousers too short even for his short legs. He sat down in the chair as if it were his own, pushed it back a little, looked straight at me, but quickly averted his eyes.

'You want me to begin?', he said, without any hesitation, as if he knew the ropes. He spoke with a foreign accent. 'I'm glad you could see me, I've heard a lot about you, people say you're good. I'll come straight to the point, and then you can sort me out.' He turned to look at me again, and I felt that his quick but penetrating glance threw down something of a challenge. But he then shifted his head, staring out of the window, and continued, less hurriedly. 'I went to this astrologer, you see, down on the pier at the seaside; I thought I'd give it a try; I'll try most things once. She asked all about my stars and so on, you know, that sort of rubbish.'

Hardly an auspicious beginning! Karl paused at his mention of the stars, as if it reminded him of something. He looked puzzled. As if to himself he said, 'Stars, moon . . . There's something back there about that.' He grimaced, and then, as if shaking it off, went on: 'She said some-thing that scared me. She said, "You've got something dark in your past, haven't you?" I don't know how she knew. I felt trapped.' Karl turned his head back and faced me. 'Can *you* read my mind?'

'Are you wishing that I could? Or are you afraid that I might?'

'I don't know.' He said this in an offhand way, as if he had not heard me properly, although his train of thought might again have switched on to something else. There was silence – a minute or two, which felt long in the circumstances – during which he appeared to go inside himself; he was looking over my shoulder, his brow wrinkled in puzzlement, his lips occasionally beginning to move as if he was wondering whether to say something. Occasionally the look of pain returned. Then, as if he had plucked up the courage to say it, Karl looked across at me again, and fixed me with his stare. 'You know, I think someone's robbed me . . .'

'Robbed you of what?'

'I don't know,' Karl replied, again in that absent-minded way.

Karl did not immediately strike me as a person whom I could help in short-term psychodynamic counselling. I was to some extent not even sure whether I liked him. His slovenly, unlooked-after appearance put me off. His attempt at familiarity ('I've heard a lot about you'), which was also perhaps a piece of flattery, did not endear him to me. His suggestion that I would 'sort him out', was a very passive way of viewing his own part in any counselling, and an exaggerated sense of the contribution which I might make. There was even a hint that he expected me to read his mind, thus totally saving him the effort of speaking his thoughts and feelings aloud.

My intervention at that point ('Or are you afraid that I might [read your mind]?') had, nonetheless, looked at an alternative explanation for his question. Yet when I had made the intervention, Karl had not appeared to take any notice of what I had said. But there again, had that question given him some impetus to look at his fear of me reading his mind? Was there something he was afraid I might find out? Some of these thoughts occurred to me at the time, and some later, as I tried to weigh up whether Karl could possibly be suitable for counselling in the short time I could offer him. Should I refer him elsewhere?

His talk about going to see an astrologer appeared to indicate that he was more persuaded by magical ideas about fate than he would be by reason and the hard work necessary for insight. On the other hand, he appeared to be wrestling with something inside himself, and this made me both more personally sympathetic to him, and more hopeful that I might help him to share some of the inner struggle. But then, having thought that, the *coup de grâce* came when he said, 'You know, I think someone's robbed me. . .' The fixed stare that accompanied the staccato sentence sounded serious warning bells for me. This, together with the anxiety about the astrologer appearing to get inside his mind, made me wonder whether Karl was paranoid. I immediately checked out the reality of the robbery – and his answer was that he did not know.

Karl's presentation was very different from Hannah's. He wanted to see me, although apparently more for what I would do for him than for the opportunity to think things through for himself. He had come of his own volition, not reluctantly at someone else's suggestion, as Hannah appeared to have done. He valued me and my skills – or at least he had said he did. Hannah had been suspicious of me and my kind. Yet for all this difference between the way in which the two of them had come to see me, I still felt much easier about the possibility of my helping Hannah than I did of being of any use to Karl. As I said to him, towards the end of that first session, I had the feeling that he was giving me a try, as he had done the astrologer, and that he might not even come back. With Hannah I had felt a willingness on her part to struggle with the difficulties she had about me: she was alert to my own contributions, and there was some rapport between us, even if at this stage it was in a delicate balance.

THE COUNSELLING SETTING

Having introduced these two contrasting clients, it might be helpful to sketch in the setting in which they were seen. Psychodynamic counselling, like other methods of counselling, needs sufficient privacy during the session to enable the client to share intimate thoughts and feelings, without fear of interruption. External intrusions are not welcomed by either the counsellor or the client. Should they occur, their effect on the client is monitored – as indeed is everything else which happens in the session. The client might, for example, feel real resentment if a telephone call is put through to the counsellor, that her time is being interrupted. But she may also feel that someone else is more important than her, and show the same signs that we might expect in sibling rivalry.

In classical analysis the patient lies on a couch, with the analyst out of sight. Many reasons for this arrangement have been given, including Freud's own remark that:

I cannot put up with being stared at by other people for eight hours a day (or more). Since, while I am listening to the patient, I too, give myself over to the current of my unconscious thoughts, I do not wish my expressions of face to give the patient material for interpretations or to influence him in what he tells me. (Quoted by Roazen, 1979: 138)

Today, particularly in counselling and shorter psychodynamic psy-chotherapy, but also in some psychoanalytic psychotherapy, both counsellor or therapist and the client sit in comfortable chairs, able to see each other, but not face to face. Eyeball to eyeball can be a very threaten-ing position, off-putting to the concentration of the client who feels even more under scrutiny; and difficult for the counsellor who wants, as Freud says above, to allow her or his own associations to spring from, and throw light upon, the client's words. Chairs are best arranged so that each can look at the other, and yet also avert their eyes without feeling too self-con-scious. The counsellor can still observe eye movements, as the reader may have noticed that I saw how Hannah and Karl shifted their gaze at differ-ent points, sometimes looking towards, sometimes away from me. In relation to the seating I also noticed how Karl had initially moved his chair back, slightly further from me, as if he did not want to sit too close. That physical movement might have been a symbolic confirmation of his concern about allowing me near his inner world.

One reason for both the couch and the invisibility of the psychoanalyst was to help the patient use the analyst as a type of 'screen', upon which to 'project' her or his imagined perceptions of the analyst. While it may be true that the less the analyst is seen the more likely are such projections to be made, I am not myself sure that the more obvious visibility of thera-pist or counsellor prevents this happening in the face-to-face seating arrangement. The psychodynamic counsellor still tends to hold back from revealing her- or himself, and so provides the opportunity for the client to imagine all manner of things about the counsellor. Of course, because the counsellor's facial expressions can be easily seen by the client, he or she has to be more careful than Freud had to be, to prevent feelings being shown – particularly those of puzzlement, worry or surprise. The ability to be 'poker-faced' is a considerable asset – although I do not mean by that a wooden appearance. Furthermore, the counsellor reveals little about her or his own private life, or personal views. Self-disclosure is debated within psychodynamic circles (e.g. in Lomas, 1973), and may not in itself discourage the type of projections and transference percep-tions through which clients 'see' their counsellor in their own particular way – as a mother or a father figure, sibling or grandparent, as disap-proving or angry – regardless of the gender, age, physical appearance, or actual expression of the counsellor. But self-disclosure is an advanced 'skill', used in such a way as not to distract the client into false views of the counsellor – Lomas, for example, notes how idealisation can follow revelation of the therapist's vulnerability (1981: 144), although this does not deter him from working with that reaction as another type of transference projection.

A psychodynamic counsellor similarly cares about the information that he or she demonstrates in the way the counselling room is set out. Although it requires comfortable and inviting furniture and decor, anything likely to provoke attention, whether a dramatic picture or curious ornament, is best avoided. I have seen displayed, in some counsellors' rooms, posters with thoughtful phrases upon them, aimed at encouraging clients to think positively, or more or less openly suggesting mottoes for looking at life. To my mind such posters and the like represent a misguided attempt to appear warm and friendly, and may even make clients wonder if they can mention the more pessimistic or even destructive thoughts which they probably have. Likewise, to display photographs of one's partner or children may attract unnecessary attention to the counsellor's family life. In making such comments I do not mean to imply that a client is not permitted to talk about the counsellor, and the counsellor's values or family, but I would always want to be sure that such questions come from the client's curiosity, and are not suggested by the surroundings. Fantasies which clients may have about the counsellor as a person can be used legitimately in psychodynamic work as ways of understanding expressions of the client's inner world, particularly when the external setting has not provided the motive or the clues for talking about them. But again this needs to be done with care: the psychodynamic approach does not employ tricks or devices, but uses what naturally arises.

The psychodynamic counsellor, like the analyst, wishes to encourage the client to speak of the ideas and images that come from within, rather than those which are suggested directly by the counsellor, or by direct stimulation of thoughts and feelings by the counsellor. It is inevitable, particularly in the early sessions, that a counsellor should do a certain amount of prompting, by asking questions, or picking up certain phrases the client has used, in order to encourage the client to expand upon allusions or hints of further information. Whenever possible, however, the counsellor who uses a psychodynamic technique prefers the client to speak of whatever comes to mind, to 'free associate', in the way Freud sketched that was quoted above. Free association does not mean a nonsensical string of words, but rather the encouragement of the client's speaking of anything that is uppermost in her or his mind. This needs to be as free as possible of the counsellor's influence; hopefully clients say what they think, and not what they think the counsellor wants them to say. The more neutral both the counsellor and the setting, the greater the possibility of the client's words being unadulterated by external stimuli.

In practice, it often requires the prompting of the counsellor for associations to take place. I have already pointed out in the last chapter, that my question to Hannah, 'What does "psychoanalyst" mean to you?' was aimed at evoking her 'associations' to that loaded term. Had I at that point ceased to be neutral, and said, 'No, I'm not', before going on to ask for her associations, my answer could have prejudiced what she said. Similarly, in that part of the session which starts this chapter, at one point I simply repeated her words, as a way of suggesting she associate to, and therefore extend, what she was saying:

Hannah: 'I didn't expect this.'

Counsellor: 'You didn't expect this.'

As I indicate below, this type of expression (reflecting back) is one of the ways of helping the client to follow a pattern of thought. Defining what the answer might be prejudices the client's subsequent reply.

It was one of Freud's analytic patients who taught him the value of paying attention to what his patients thought, rather than pursuing his own particular line of questioning. Roazen (1979: 98–9) records how this happened:

> [Freud's] account of how he adopted the technique of free association is touching . . . in its simplicity. A patient appears to have stoutly resisted Freud's interfering with the flow of the clinical material. 'I now saw that I had gained nothing by this interruption and that I cannot evade listening to her stories in every detail to the very end.' At another point the same patient 'said in a definitely grumbling tone that I was to stop keep on asking her where this or that comes from, but to let her tell me what she had to say.' As Freud quietly put it, 'I fell in with this . . .'. (For the original account, see Freud and Breuer, 1895: 119–20)

The similarity between Freud's discovery and the person-centred approach later advocated by Carl Rogers is obvious. (See the companion volume in this series by Mearns and Thorne (1988).) I suspect that the more Freud understood about the workings of the human personality, and the causes of particular problems, the more difficult it was for him to stop explaining to his patients what was wrong with them. This is a perennial problem for the psychodynamic counsellor, because the more he or she learns from and about clients, the more tempting it is to anticipate what each new client has to discover for her- or himself. The complex psychological theory that accompanies the psychodynamic approach should in fact warn the counsellor against making assumptions about clients. Nevertheless, there is pressure in the counselling room for answers, particularly from some demanding or distressed clients. At such times it is tempting for the counsellor to use theoretical knowledge, to gratify the curiosity, or to try to assuage the distress of the client, but doing so always carries the risk of imposing solutions, rather than following the much more open (if also more fraught) way of following the client's agenda and the client's own thought and feelings. In that respect psychodynamic counselling is very definitely client-centred.

SOME BASIC TECHNIQUES

Apart from providing a setting which is as far as possible neutral enough to ensure the true freedom of a client's associations, what contribution can the counsellor make to assist clients in 'telling their story', and developing their own associations? Since I have written at length elsewhere (Jacobs, 1999) about the essential basic guidelines which a counsellor uses, there is no need to repeat them in detail. Such guidelines (sometimes called micro-skills) apply equally well to other counselling approaches (such as person-centred or humanistic), and need not be thought of as peculiarly psychodynamic, even though some of them are clearly in evidence in Freud's early case-histories. These basic skills provide an essential basis for the more distinctive psychodynamic interventions used by the counsellor, which I describe in later chapters. Here I describe them briefly, to show how the psychodynamic approach consists of much more than a series of interpretations. I adopt a slightly different scheme here for defining the basic listening and responding techniques used by the counsellor, and dividing the basic skills into six categories.

Listening and Observing

It almost goes without saying that a counsellor needs to listen carefully to what the client says. Listening takes place at different levels: first, listening to the actual words, the factual information, as well as minute details such as choice of expression, and even the misuse of words, such as in the famous Freudian slip. Such detailed listening notes the way in which a client might begin a word, only to change it to another, censoring the first one which had come to mind. It includes noticing words which can be interpreted in more than one sense, because the alternative meaning might also be significant. For instance, when Karl told me that he had heard I was 'good', I first thought he intended to flatter me as a counsellor; but I wondered afterwards whether it was a moral quality to which he alluded, which made him put me up on a pedestal, contrasted with the 'dark in his past'.

Secondly, the counsellor also needs to listen to the mood, the feeling, and the underlying messages that are conveyed through the actual words that the client chooses. Listening in this way is like listening to the bass line of a piece of music, and helps the counsellor to identify feelings and thoughts which the client seems to have experienced, but is unable to put into actual words – perhaps because the client does not like to admit certain feelings either to her- or himself, or to the counsellor.

Listening in this careful way, with attention to what the client is actually saying, and probably implying, helps the counsellor also to remember more than we often can in two-way conversations, which is important because it is not possible to comment on everything the client says. At times a client will be in full flow, and the counsellor does not wish to interrupt. Points that might have been taken up, or questions that might have been asked, therefore have to be held in abeyance and in memory. Nor is it always possible to understand the meaning of some parts or phrases in the client's story, so the counsellor has to hold those aspects in mind, until the client later says something that perhaps throws light on unclear areas. By holding on to the client's unfolding story and associations to it, the counsellor looks for threads that run through, from which he or she might then weave an overall response, that both summarises what the client has been expressing, and hopefully highlights what may be the most significant features.

Listening and remembering has to be supplemented by watching closely for the client's non-verbal communication and reactions. For example, I had noticed the way in which Hannah initially sat perched on the edge of her chair, while Karl had moved the chair further away. Karl had shifted his gaze away from me, matching his hesitancy about sitting too close. Hannah had looked angrily at me, before she fired her first question, in that instance her tone of voice matching her expression. Sometimes non-verbal communication, through gestures, posture or facial expression, reveals a feeling which is not being expressed so clearly through tone of voice or choice of words.

There is a third aspect to listening, which Freud alluded to in the reference earlier: '. . . while I am listening to the patient, I too, give myself over to the current of my unconscious thoughts.' The counsellor thus listens to her- or himself, to what the counsellor is feeling about the client, and about aspects of the client's story. Indeed, the counsellor even listens to those apparently extraneous thoughts that come to mind, which sometimes prove to be more relevant than at first might seem possible.

Listening to oneself is also the first stage of empathising, or identifying with the client. Psychodynamic theory suggests that the ability to empathise, or to identify with how others might be feeling, is one which develops from the intimate relationship of mother and baby, each understanding intuitively how the other might be feeling. Empathy, or identification, means the ability to put oneself into someone's shoes, to get into their skin, to experience what they might be experiencing. There is, however, a difference between empathy and sympathy.

Empathy describes the ability to *perceive* what another person might be feeling, whether or not in those circumstances the counsellor would her- or himself feel the same way. Sympathy means to *experience* the same feelings that the other person has. The ability to sympathise often forms a good starting point for empathy (as long as we do not confuse our own feelings with the other person's). Yet it is not necessary to be sympathetic to a person in order to be empathic. I had felt little sympathy in myself for Karl at the start of the interview – but this did not prevent me from trying to identify what he might be experiencing. On the other hand, despite her initial hostility, I felt more sympathetic towards Hannah, experiencing in myself some of the sadness which Hannah displayed at the point above at which we left her. It is important, however, to bear in mind that listening to oneself should not lead to the imposition of one's ideas and feelings on the client. The counsellor's feelings and associations always need checking out with all that the client has been expressing.

These different levels of listening and observation demand much of the counsellor. If the counsellor is to attend carefully to what is said and not said, and to make sense of the material, it is essential that he or she hold back from saying too much, because the more he or she gets drawn into a to-and-fro conversation, the harder it is to concentrate upon the client. Wherever possible the counsellor avoids saying anything just for the sake of it, although I would not go so far as Langs (as cited by Grant, 1984: 334) in suggesting that the therapist should say nothing until he is ninety-five per cent sure that what he says is going to be right. Nevertheless, he or she remains relatively silent, particularly until it is clear that the client has finished speaking, and is looking for the counsellor's response. When the response is given it is more often than not fairly minimal, a few words that simply nudge the client into saying more. The counsellor's silence generally assists the client's free association. Holding back by the counsellor is not done to frustrate or anger clients, nor to make them feel uncomfortable. It is rather a sign of the respect which the counsellor has for the client setting the agenda, and leading the way. In the examples given of the opening moments with both Karl and Hannah, I therefore said nothing when they first came in, not even to introduce myself (although this might be helpful). I waited for them to start. From the outset, what matters to the client is more important than what the counsellor wants to know. Often a non-verbal gesture is sufficient, indicating that the floor is theirs.

The reader may also have noticed a silence after Karl's opening comments, which was in fact one or two minutes in length. To a new client such a silence may seem very long, and the counsellor has to gauge whether to break the tension of it, or whether the client is thinking something out. In the latter case interruption of the silence is obviously always helpful or sensitive to where the client wishes to be. Later, as the client gets more used to the way the counsellor allows silences, a counsellor needs to detect what mood accompanies a period of quietness. Both the non-verbal communication, and the empathic listening by the counsellor, can help suggest what might be being expressed in the silence. During the silence that occurred in Karl's session, I was able to observe his own internal tussle over what he should say next. The silence also gave me space to develop a possible intervention should it seem called for. In the event, any interruption of the silence by me was unnecessary because Karl broke it, with his dramatic statement about being robbed. A different situation arose in the session with Hannah, where the silence was very brief, and I added a tentative explanation about her wish to go on seeing her doctor, which appeared to help her say something about her perception of herself.

The apparently passive role of listening is in fact a very active one. In the counsellor's mind there are a hundred and one words, signals, cues and hints of which he or she tries to make some sense and order. Good listening, and the ability simultaneously to reflect on what the client conveys, help the counsellor, as and when it seems appropriate, to make relevant and careful responses.

Reflecting Responses

There is one type of response which is especially useful for moving the client's story along, and which has the added bonus that it helps the counsellor find more space, to dwell on what the client is trying to express. This response is to reflect back to the client, either briefly, or by paraphrase and précis, what the client has been saying. It indicates to the client that the counsellor has been listening; it helps the counsellor check that what he or she has heard is accurate; and it often helps the client to develop what he or she was saying.

Reflecting responses can be made by a straightforward repetition of words: 'You didn't expect this,' I had said to Hannah, virtually repeating her own phrase. Reflecting can take the form of a paraphrase: 'You hoped you'd be able to talk to a woman,' I had said, again to Hannah. Reflecting can also be done through a rhetorical question, which in effect repeats the client's last few words, and begs the answer 'Yes' or 'No' . For instance, I could have said to Hannah, 'You didn't expect this?' – that is, I could have asked a question. I would have expected the answer 'No', but I would have also hoped for further explanation. A response which reflects back needs to be as accurate as possible, catching the right tone and mood of the client's words, as well as their content.

Exploratory Responses

Exploratory responses should also be accurate, although by their very nature they cannot be as accurate as reflecting responses, because there is inevitably a tentative quality to them. The exploratory response attempts to draw out something extra from the client, which he or she is not obviously saying in words, but which may be hinted at, in tone of voice, or by non-verbal expression. So, again drawing upon the part of the session with Hannah which heads this chapter, the counsellor may observe a feeling which is being expressed facially: 'You look rather sad'; or may draw out a 'bass line' (as in music) feeling: 'You wanted to go on seeing your doctor?'

Another example is the empathic response, which tries to put into words what the counsellor thinks the client might currently be feeling or have experienced at the time of the events which are being talked about: 'That sounds confusing for you.' There is more risk in making such exploratory responses: first, because the counsellor may not be correct in her or his perception; and secondly, because the counsellor needs to gauge whether the client is ready to accept something which has not been directly expressed. Sometimes the counsellor is correct, but nevertheless premature in giving voice to a hidden feeling, which leads the client to deny it – either refusing to recognise such a feeling, or unable to own it in front of the counsellor. For this reason, and because of the tentative quality of exploratory responses, they are best expressed with some form of qualification, such as: 'Perhaps, I wonder if, I am guessing but I think, maybe, could it be? etc.' For example, I had suggested to Hannah, 'Perhaps it's difficult to tell me because I'm a man.'

Information-seeking Responses

Another type of response is one which is aimed at clarification, usually expressed in the form of a question, seeking to elicit more information, either of an isolated fact, or of the broader sweep of events. Information-seeking responses are obviously more frequently used in the first, or early sessions, when the counsellor is trying to build up a picture of the client's background and history. Questions begin to give way to other types of response, except at those times when questions are necessary for pieces of information which the counsellor feels might be helpful. Very occasionally, especially when the counsellor is unsure of the suitability of a client, questions are put which seek very specific answers, for example, to make important clarification of the seriousness of disturbing feelings, or of the risk of danger to the client or others. Questions aimed at finding out facts tend to be closed, seeking a specific piece of information. Those that provide more scope for alternative answers, or wider dimensions of a subject tend to be open questions. My closed question to Karl, 'Robbed of what?', was an attempt to clarify whether he was speaking of an external event, which (were it so) would have made me less concerned about the presence of paranoid feelings in him. In circumstances where I was less puzzled or concerned about his mental state, I could have said nothing, waiting for the client to expand on his remark; or I could have simply responded, 'Robbed?', as much a reflecting as an information-seeking response.

Too often the standard response of caring professionals, such as doctors, lawyers and social workers, is to ask a whole series of questions. Of course, they nearly always need specific information in order to provide their help, and precise questions appear to further that end. By contrast, counsellors have more time to offer their clients, and are interested in more than factual information, so they do not have to ask so many questions, or if they ask questions, they make efforts to avoid the interaction becoming like a formal interview.

Yet psychodynamic counsellors have a certain problem. On the one hand, they do not want to appear over-zealous in their questioning; on the other, they find knowledge of the client's history useful in formulating their interpretations. Some analysts and psychotherapists (like some psychiatrists and psychologists) like to take a formal history before starting therapy. This necessitates a change of style on the part of the therapist, once the history-taking is completed, to which the patient has to get accustomed. Many other therapists and counsellors prefer to help clients relate their history at their own pace, although perhaps with rather more interruptions for particular pieces of information in the first two or three sessions than the person-centred counsellor (for example) might make. It is possible for any counsellor to find out a considerable amount of background information in the first session, without obviously asking a series of questions. Interruptions of the client for specific information may need to be followed by helping the client to get back to what he or she was talking about. The next part of Hannah's first session of counselling illustrates how this may be done.

WHAT BROUGHT HANNAH FOR COUNSELLING

Hannah did not cry for long; indeed she began to show signs of impatience with herself, I thought, although it might have been impatience with me. She sat back in the chair, sighed deeply, and began to talk about herself, and what had taken her to see the doctor:

'You're right. I'm fed up with looking after other people – I've spent my whole life doing it, and it's about time I had a break. It's been one thing after another, as long as I can remember, although I suppose I didn't notice it so much when I was younger.'

'What age are you now?'

'I'm 23. I feel I've lived a lot longer than that.'

The danger of any question is that it changes the topic, or introduces new material which leads a client away from the subject which he or she has introduced. Hannah had touched on an important feeling, but I had interrupted her to get some information that I thought might be useful. (Having got her present age, allusions to other dates or years of her life might not require further questions.) I therefore wanted to help her get back to what she was saying.

'You were saying that you didn't notice looking after people so much when you were younger.'

'No . . . I loved my grandfather. He was all I had; I suppose I thought he looked after me.'

'He was all you had?'

'Yes, well my mother died when I was tiny – and I never knew my father – my grandfather hasn't got a good word to say for him. Strikes me they're all the same . . . my brother must take after my father.' She paused. 'Granddad says I'm like my mother.' The last words were said wistfully.

Before she spoke about her likeness to her mother, Hannah had been getting quite worked up. There were as yet many questions in my mind, although I had already learned a lot: she had not known her parents, she had lost her mother when she was small (but how small?); her father was no good (in what way?); her brother was the same (was he older or younger?); her grandfather was still alive. Although she had expressed a lot of closeness to him, she had said that she 'loved' him (in the past tense, as if there were different feelings for him now). It can be seen how her history had built up quite rapidly, without my having to ask too many formal or 'closed' questions.

She went on, putting the brief mention of mother to one side. 'I thought Kit might be different – he seemed to be so kind. He didn't say a lot. He'd just listen to me when I was down. I didn't think that he'd drop us in it.'

'Kit?'

'He's a friend . . . well, I thought he was a friend. Not a boyfriend you know, I don't want that. Granddad takes all my time. He's still trying to adjust to leaving London.'

'London?'

'Well, it's a long story. I don't know if I've got time . . .'

Hannah stopped. I wasn't sure whether she wanted to tell me any more, or whether her temporary trust in me, during which she had shared a number of potentially highly emotional pieces of information, had been checked by her mention of Kit. I could not pursue her history any more for the time being, and decided instead to look at her anxiety about talking in this way to me.

'We do have another forty minutes, and I think for my part that it might be helpful to meet again. You've told me a lot already. It seems as if you have lost so much in the past: your mother, your home in London, Kit's friendship, something about your grandfather that you've lost too. And when you went to see the doctor you felt she didn't have time, and I think you felt you had lost her when she suggested you see me. But I'm wondering now whether you think I could be like Kit, someone who doesn't say much, someone who listens to you, but someone who might drop you in it, and let you down?'

'Yes, I don't know what to make of you. There have been so many rotten men before now, even the ones I thought were all right. I don't know whether you're any different.'

Linking Responses: Towards Interpretation

This last, and longer, intervention of mine was another type of response. It linked several words or phrases which Hannah had said, and it included a tentative interpretation to try to help her understand the anxiety she may have felt in talking to me. This type of intervention illustrates a type of response, which I classify as more than a basic technique, although it is fundamental to psychodynamic counselling. It is a more advanced skill, which is more readily learned once a trainee counsellor has had both some experience of, and acquired sufficient confidence in the basic techniques. The linking and interpretative intervention is to some extent a development of the empathic response: that response which tries to highlight half-expressed or implied feelings and thoughts. There is, however, a difference in that an empathic response points to a conscious or semi-conscious feeling, of which a client is aware, although cannot verbalise to her- or himself or to the counsellor. An interpretative response is aimed more at elucidating unconscious feelings or ideas, of which the client is perhaps unaware. A skilful interpretation observes feelings and ideas which are close enough to the surface, and allows them to enter into consciousness. A badly timed interpretation, however accurate it seems, is often resisted, because the client is not ready to hear it.

Making links in the client's story is a more simple kind of interpretation. An example of bringing together different elements occurred when I said to Hannah, 'On the one hand you're not sure you can speak to me; but part of you wants someone to pay attention to what you're feeling; and then again you aren't sure you have got any value compared to other people . . .' On their own, each of these statements is a straightforward reflection of things Hannah has said. Juxtaposed, they express one of the conflicts she was experiencing on an unconscious level.

Linking apparently disparate sentences in a person's story, done well, can reunite split off or separated feelings, which the client has been unable to acknowledge as belonging together. Conflicting feelings easily cause the type of tension which leads to emotional disturbance. In Hannah's more detailed story of what had been happening to her, there were some hints at what might make it difficult for her to acknowledge how much she wanted to be cared for. She seemed afraid that expressing this need to anyone would lead to disappointment, which Kit, and perhaps her grandfather, seemed to have given her. She therefore adopted the position of being the one who cared for others, this being a safer way of relating to others than expecting care from them. But I felt that Hannah had conflicting feelings

43

about Kit and her grandfather, even though I was not absolutely sure what they were, or how they had come about.

Every counsellor has to make some kind of assessment about the suitability of a new client for the approach he or she uses. It is important, for instance, that the client responds well to the basic techniques – that the client takes some initiative for speaking, and does not rely on the counsellor for advice or solutions. To make good use of the psychodynamic approach, the client needs to show some insight (understanding) of her or himself, and also to respond thoughtfully (although not compliantly) to linking responses and interpretations. Therefore, in the first session, it is useful to make at least one 'trial' interpretation, albeit a tentative one, to assess whether the client responds to the counsellor's insight, perhaps by showing in return some of their own. My 'trial' interpretation to Hannah ran: 'I'm wondering now whether you think I could be like Kit, someone who doesn't say much, someone who listens to you, but someone who might drop you in it, and let you down?' Hannah's reply showed that she was able to hear what I had said, and develop it for herself. Her hostility and suspicion were nowhere near as marked as they had been in the opening moments of the session.

Frieda Fromm-Reichmann succinctly sums up what interpretation tries to do:

> Interpretation means translating into the language of awareness, and thereby bringing into the open, what the patient communicates, with [the patient] being conscious of its contents, its dynamics, its revealing connections with other experiences, or the various implications pertaining to its factual or emotional background. (Singer, 1965: 199)

Interpretation can be made of the client's material, without explicit reference to the counselling relationship (see Chapter 4); or of the defences and resistance which the counsellor detects in the client (see Chapter 5); or of the transference relationship to the counsellor (see Chapter 6). I made an early tentative interpretation about Hannah's fears of the transference relationship between herself and me ('You're afraid I will only be interested in sex') – linking me by implication to the reference to men in general and Freud in particular which Hannah had voiced. There is a similar attempt to bring the relationship between Karl and myself into focus, with a half empathic, half interpretative question, when I asked whether he was afraid that I might read his mind. His response to this was noncommittal. It made me wonder whether I would be able to use a psychodynamic approach with him, although my remark was too imprecise for me to make an adequate assessment on one intervention alone.

Informing Responses

In addition to reflecting, observing, questioning and linking responses, there is a final category, which consists of interventions which impart information to the client. Clarification by the counsellor is sometimes important as well as helpful: 'No, I'm a counsellor' seemed a necessary statement after I had explored what Hannah had meant by 'psychoanalyst'. In the latter part of the session described above I gave her clear information about the length of time we had left in the session, which Hannah needed to know. Another type of information, which a counsellor sometimes gives, is a rather more general or theoretical explanation of a person's feelings or behaviour. This is something which Freud appears to have done quite frequently in his own practice, hoping (rather too optimistically, as he admitted later) that rational explanation would assist the patient to give up neurotic traits. Rational explanation, when given, is no substitute for insight – the latter term being more akin to 'personal awareness' than intellectual knowledge.

Finally, there are occasions when a counsellor feels it is appropriate to give advice, or even a clear instruction. An example of advice appears in my longer intervention in Hannah's session: 'I think for my part that it might be helpful to meet again.' An example of instruction, later used with Karl, was: 'I'd like you to see your doctor and tell him that you are seeing me, so that he knows what is happening.' As with other information-giving responses, advice and instruction are not very frequently used, but at times can be essential in assisting clients to manage some aspect of their lives, or in helping to create a reasonable level of coping with outside factors to enable 'inner work' to go on.

TOUCH AND ABSTINENCE

The psychodynamic approach to counselling is a highly verbal one, although not as cerebral and intellectual as it is sometimes thought. Responses and interpretations are aimed at feeling as well as at thinking, at what is conscious and what is currently unconscious. It is not the aim of psychodynamic work, as it occasionally appears to be the case in Freud's work, to conquer 'passion by reason' (Fromm, 1959: 93). But neither is reason scorned, even if rationalisation is recognised as a defence (see Chapter 5).

Psychodynamic counselling encourages full expression of thought, fantasy and feeling. Yet 'full expression' is limited to the verbal. Physical expression (excepting, of course, non-verbal communication such as tears, or involuntary bodily movement such as banging a hand on the arm of the chair) is discouraged. Both 'acting out', which I explain in the next chapter, and its equivalent within the session, 'acting in', are felt to prevent the full expression of feeling and fantasy.

This may sound severe, but it in effect means that the client is not expected to throw things, break up the room, or physically attack or cling to the counsellor. *Verbal expressions* of various wishes, such as clinging to, or hugging the counsellor, or smashing the window or the counsellor's face, are the only permitted way of showing such intense feelings; and such putting of feelings into words is not in the least discouraged. Psychodynamic counselling might be likened to the theatrical stage, as opposed to the film set. In the theatre emotions are expressed through words, and rarely in action (actions tend to take place off-stage). On the film set emotions are conveyed as much by action as by words. The film set, or off-stage, is the client's life outside the counselling session. On stage, in the counselling room, the vocabulary can be very rich and equally expressive, the air can go blue with rage or red hot with passion, but the expression of feelings is confined nonetheless to words.

It is rare that a counsellor actually has to delineate such boundaries. Most clients only dream of acting in such ways towards their therapist or counsellor. The expectation that feelings will be put into words is conveyed through the counsellor's own behaviour. So, when I felt for Hannah in her sadness, I made no attempt to comfort her as I might have done had she been one of my family or a close friend. This is another aspect of the 'rule of abstinence' referred to in the previous chapter.

There are several other reasons for not touching the client. First, although the counsellor does not glory in other people suffering, it is not necessarily helpful to alleviate pain prematurely, before the full force of the feelings has been expressed. Rather than suppress, or even deny the opportunity for expression of feelings, a counsellor hopes that expression of pain may lead to some release (as crying can often help alleviate distress) as well as more understanding of what is causing such hurt. Had I therefore, through my words (let alone touch), comforted Hannah at the point at which she looked sad, I could easily have prevented the material emerging to which she gave expression in both her tears and her words.

Sometimes this means that a counsellor has to stand inactively by, sympathetically but silently, while a client works through the expression of their pain. This is where the empathic response is so crucial, staying with the pain of the client, but indicating by words and tone of voice just how much the counsellor appreciates what the client is going through.

A second reason for not touching is that such a movement towards the client, however well-meant, can easily be taken as threatening. Hannah had clearly expressed her hostility towards men who see sex in everything, and I had every reason to think that movement towards her, perhaps even of verbal comfort, would be interpreted by her as a threat, as if I too were only after sex. It did not matter that my own feeling for her at that point was more maternal than sexual. Hannah (and indeed many other clients) could easily have misinterpreted a gentle hand as an unwelcome physical intrusion. This is particularly important when we bear in mind just how many clients may have suffered sexual or physical abuse at some time. Physical closeness may be terrifying for them, although the compliant manner they have been forced to adopt as victims may not allow them to express their concern at a counsellor who tries to be comforting in the wrong way. I would go so far as to express some reservation about shaking hands with a person at the end of every session, although this may of course happen at the end of a first or a last session. This is not because shaking hands is a sexual gesture, but because it is a social convention of which one meaning is making peace with each other. If shaking hands prevents the client expressing that he or she is still angry with me, or thinks that I have been made angry by them, then I would sooner it did not happen.

A third reason for avoiding touch in counselling is that to some clients it may appear to encourage an attachment to the counsellor (whether of a 'mother–baby' sort or of a sexual kind) which they desperately want, but which should never be deliberately fostered. Such attachments are formed by certain clients readily enough, without the counsellor having to provoke them. If they then occur, the counsellor can more reliably ascribe them to the needs and wishes of the client, than to any provocation of such feelings by the counsellor's physical approach.

FROM FIRST IMPRESSIONS TO FINDING A FOCUS

It is clear from the many considerations in this chapter that the first session is a very full one for the counsellor – perhaps more so than any other session. Apart from practising the basic techniques of counselling, designed to help the client to speak more freely, the counsellor needs to clarify any doubts there may be about the suitability of the client for psychodynamic counselling, to test out whether the client can use interpretations, and to see whether the transference relationship will be a help rather than a hindrance. In addition, the counsellor wishes to form a general picture of the client, with, if possible, a definite focus for her or his interventions. How the psychodynamic counsellor approaches this task is explained in the next chapter.

3

AFTER THE FIRST SESSION

RECORDING THE SESSION

There are different methods that can be used to record what happens and what is said in any counselling session. Whichever method is chosen, it serves several purposes: one is to make a clear record to assist the counsellor in remembering what the client (and the counsellor) said. I have already emphasised how important remembering detail is for building up a fuller picture of the client, and formulating dynamic ideas about how the client reacts to different situations. A second, equally valuable reason for remembering as much as possible is that clients tend to appreciate a counsellor who shows that he or she has been listening, and can recall things that were said perhaps weeks ago.

A third reason for having a good method of recording is to enable the counsellor to use such information in supervision. In that context a detailed account allows the counsellor to convey what each person said, how one response led to another; to recall the non-verbal communication shown by the client and the counsellor's own thoughts as the session proceeded. The fuller this account, the more the supervisor can appreciate what the original counselling work might have been like, even though it is difficult to be accurate without listening to a whole tape of a session. Inevitably, supervision tends to be a selective look at any one or more sessions. With detailed information, both technique and psychodynamic understanding can be discussed in supervision.

However, supervision normally only gives enough space to look at the counsellor's work with one or two clients at a time, especially when the counsellor is more experienced and prefers to concentrate upon one client in order to maximise the ongoing learning opportunities. A good method of recording should be able to assist counsellors to reflect upon their other clients as well, not just in respect of factual information, but as a means of taking a broader view of the psychodynamic picture built up over a period of time with the client. Since it is not possible to record every session in detail (except with tapes, but even then it is impossible to hear them all played back!), it is important to develop a method which allows brief, but significant notes to be made.

The discipline of reflecting upon sessions enables a counsellor to move gradually from a bird's-eye view after each session, to looking at what might be going on in the course of the session. Just as counselling itself aims to extend the client's changing feelings and attitudes within the session to more general application in 'the outside world', so supervision and good recording move the process of reflecting upon a single example of work, to a continuous internalised appraisal of oneself, and of one's skills and ability to understand the client.

The Use of Tapes

The methods of recording that are open to the psychodynamic counsellor are no different from those in use by other types of counsellor. The use of audio- or video-tape has some advantages, in that it presents a very accurate record of the session. Since a counsellor's memory is bound to be selective, as well as at times faulty, sometimes only remembering what he or she wants to, as well as often forgetting certain pieces of information, taping is a good check upon what was actually said by each person. I once felt taping was extremely intrusive, but I have come round to appreciate its value, particularly in the detailed supervision of a person's work. Audio-tape (and less likely because of its more obvious presence, video-tape) is a useful adjunct for training, where time spent in detailed analysis of the whole or parts of a session is re-paid in the quality of later work.

There are disadvantages in the use of the technical equipment necessary for taping. The record that tape provides may be a full one, but in one sense it is too full, because playing back a whole session takes as long as the original 'hour', and extends both the time necessary for supervision and a counsellor's own time in reflection. It is useful for reflecting upon one or two clients when in training, but in a busy counselling practice it is impracticable to play every tape back.

A further difficulty in using technical equipment is the effect which it may have on the client (as well perhaps as on the counsellor). Permission must be sought, but even if it is freely given, adopting a psychodynamic approach means taking into account the impact of every factor present in a session. A number of questions arise therefore in relation to the taping of sessions: What does a microphone or a camera add to the counselling session? What fantasies are created in the mind of the client? Does the potential use of this material elsewhere appeal to the exhibitionism of some people, or strengthen the inhibitions of others? What effect does taping have on the spontaneity, not only of the client but also of the counsellor? Does a client agree to the use of tape out of deference to the counsellor? Finally, because the psychodynamic approach listens in the detail for oblique references to feelings and thoughts, is the counsellor prepared to treat the taping itself as yet another factor to which the client may unconsciously or obliquely refer?

Since remembering and reflecting during the actual counselling session is so important, it is also important to bear in mind that using tapes may sometimes impede the development of the counsellor's memory, which must be trained for as accurate a recall as possible, since what is said at the start of a session may need to be referred back to towards the end of a session; the tape cannot be re-played at that point! A trainee eventually has to move from the luxury of detailed analysis to the more crowded timetable of the counselling practice, where the vagaries of memory take over from the machine. The better training the memory has been given, the greater use can be made of all the details which go to make up any counselling session.

THE VERBATIM

A second method of recording, which is likewise valuable in training, as well as in ongoing supervision, is writing out the content of the counselling session in as much detail as possible, including not only the words spoken but other observations, as well. To complete such a task takes almost as long as the session itself (and therefore has limitations such as those outlined above), although it has the advantage of helping to develop the counsellor's memory. Such a verbatim account can never be as accurate, word for word, as taping is, but it can include thoughts and associations which passed through the counsellor's mind, which tapes cannot record. While there are bound to be gaps in the counsellor's remembering, such 'missing links' may in themselves prove significant if they are subsequently recalled – 'why did I forget such an important phrase, or event, which the client spoke about?' These lapses sometimes occur because the counsellor was not fully listening, or found what the client was saying difficult to understand, or because the counsellor's responding was less than helpful. In supervision, gaps in the verbatim record can sometimes be looked at more carefully, in case they indicate something potentially important about the client or the session. Often a supervisor's comments or questions help the counsellor to remember further material not recorded at the time.

A PSYCHODYNAMIC STRUCTURE FOR RECORDING

A third way of recording the session is to make shorter notes, which are structured enough to assist the counsellor's reflection, and serve as an *aide-mémoire* for future sessions. There is no standard method by which psychodynamic counsellors make notes on their sessions, and each counsellor needs to develop her or his own system, since the type of information a counsellor wishes to use in subsequent sessions varies. The structure of recording which I outline is one which I have myself continuously adapted over many years, having taken the original form from Balint's account of assessment interviews (Balint et al., 1972). In reproducing it I suggest only a model which other psychodynamic counsellors may wish to adapt for their own purposes. At the same time the structure of this method of recording suggests for the trainee in psychodynamic counselling the main considerations which a psychodynamic counsellor has in mind, in trying to understand the client, in assessing the suitability of the client for the psychodynamic approach, and in reflecting upon the client after the session.

In the recording structure that follows I can include more details of the first two sessions with Hannah, one of the clients previously mentioned. I later come back to the other client, Karl, to illustrate how such a record also assists assessment of a client's suitability for psychodynamic counselling. This particular method of recording allows the counsellor to add new material and possible insights in an ordered way after each session. It is doubtful whether the first session in itself provides enough information with which to understand the client, although in my experience it often turns out that everything that is important to the client is present in the first session, even if often in an embryonic or obscure form. Later sessions clarify the issues, although they often demonstrate that the client in one sense 'said it all' during the first meeting.

It needs to be stressed that the way in which a psychodynamic counsellor approaches recording means that it is a tentative aid for the counsellor, and not an infallible picture of the client. The counsellor uses notes as 'scribblings' or 'sketches', and as a means of suggesting possibilities, which always need testing out by listening carefully to the client before they move beyond the status of 'hunches'. Some of the hunches are never tested in a particular piece of counselling, because the client chooses to concentrate upon certain features in her or his life and feels no need to look at deeper or different issues. Even those ideas which are more relevant to the client's particular agenda have to be used carefully. It is certainly not wise to push bright ideas at a client simply on the strength of a supervisor's suggestions, or as a result of the counsellor's spotting possibilities while writing up after the last session. The counsellor has to wait to see what the client wants to express, and to wait both for an opportunity and for confirmation that afterthoughts might be relevant. Both notes and supervision enable ideas to be stored away, waiting for the time to come when the client either suggests similar ideas, or provides an opening for a tentative intervention.

My 'notes' on Hannah were not actually written down during the session – this would be distracting, not to say anxiety-provoking, to the client. They represent the ideas that occurred to me during and after the first two sessions. They were only tentative, sparked off by the relationship and by some of the things that Hannah said; but they formed a series of working hypotheses, which remained to be tested, and were open to change and development in the light of further information. The headings are standard to my notes. The sections in italics refer to Hannah, although I also include comments to explain the meaning of each heading and its significance in building up a psychodynamic picture of the client, and of the counselling possibilities.

HANNAH: NOTES ON THE FIRST TWO SESSIONS

One record sheet is reserved for the factual material that I learn from the client as the sessions progress. To facilitate the reader's understanding of the inevitably shorthand notes that follow the factual material, I therefore include this first; and in the headings that follow the factual material I draw out the possible significance of the information I learned about Hannah.

Factual material

Session 1: *Moved from London in January – evicted from house and shop – grandfather owned antique business, but over recent years has been gambling heavily and lost all his money. Debts on accommodation led to eviction, loss of home: now living in small rented flat with him. Has job in office as clerk; but hardly enough earnings to keep both of them.*

Family: *Elder brother, not living at home, has in past lived off them without contributing much himself. Mother died when client few weeks old; father had died around same time. Grandfather brought up client and brother. Mother's mother had also died, in childbirth, and mother had been brought up by grandfather. Grandfather heartbroken by both deaths, initially lavished care on client, but had become more demanding during her teens.*

Session 2: *Eviction, landlord had threatened for long time and tried bargaining with client – would let them stay in return for sexual favours. Brother too had tried to 'make match' between client and his best friend. Client has male friend, Kit, to whom very attached (non sexual), but felt let down by him – Kit first broke news to her of grandfather's gambling habits. (And she thinks Kit 'split' on them to landlord.) Out at night recently, and saw shadowy figure in back street, same build as landlord. Dreamed that he must have followed them to this town, that he still determined to 'have' her as payment for debts.*

More about family: *Grandfather had younger brother who had gone abroad many years ago – only other surviving relative.*

The factual information is also translated into the 'family tree' below (p. 60). Generally, the amount of fresh historical material diminishes as the sessions progress, becoming easier to record. I would normally include current events (such as thinking she saw the landlord in the street) in the sessional themes (see below), but I include it here to provide a fuller picture for what follows.

54

Presenting Problems and Duration

(a) Depressed (four weeks)
(b) Relationship difficulties with men (? years)

By 'presenting problems' I mean those presented by the client at the first session. Other problems that may emerge in later sessions can be included either in this section or the section below on 'Further Problems'. The presenting problems, together with their duration, provide an opportunity to assess whether counselling is the appropriate method of help, and which of the presenting problems are going to form the main focus of the counsellor's attention. In Hannah's case her depression appeared to be of recent origin, and the problem of relating to men (which arose incidentally through having to see a male counsellor for the first session, but nonetheless seemed a significant one to me) was one of indeterminate duration. The psychodynamic approach was appropriate to both these problems, but longer-term therapy rather than counselling would have been more suitable for the second difficulty, because it appeared to have been an area of concern for much longer. As I suggest later, the duration of a symptom or a problem is one factor in determining whether counselling or psychotherapy should be offered, if the choice is available.

Precipitating Factors

Moving from London ten weeks ago, after eviction. Although appears to have become depressed six weeks later: delayed reaction? Or some other factor? In second session told me of seeing silhouette of someone at night, which reminded her of former landlord.

What is it about this point of time that brings the client to the counsellor (or to the person who referred the client for counselling)? Why now, rather than at some earlier time? These are significant questions for the psychodynamic counsellor, who wishes to understand what it was that triggered a client's reaction, since the trigger is sometimes a repetition of an unresolved difficulty from the past. Hannah, for instance, seemed to cope with the eviction for six weeks before becoming depressed. Was she only able to allow herself to feel depressed after she and her grandfather had settled down in their new flat? On occasion, external reality issues can keep psychological problems at bay, and only as the external situation eases do accompanying emotional factors come to the fore. After the first session

I was uncertain about the trigger for her depression, although in the second session she had told me about the silhouette which had frightened her. The meaning to her of that particular incident did not emerge until a later session (see Chapter 5).

Current Conflicts (and Further Problems)

(a) Feelings towards grandfather – grateful for his care of her as child, but resents his clinging to her now.

(b) Wants independence from grandparent, but still wanting her own dependent needs to be met at home?

(c) Difficult to leave grandfather, because of guilt about her angry feelings towards him?

Much of the stress caused by current (or past) events arises (or arose) from the conflict between different, often opposite, feelings. Included in this section, therefore, are current feelings which appear to be in conflict. The client may describe such feelings quite clearly or the counsellor may infer them from different expressions used by the client. The second and third conflicts are ideas which I had, which I therefore recorded with a question mark, because at this early stage they were still 'hunches'.

It is not unusual for clients to tell the counsellor later about problems other than those they mentioned in the first session. While psychodynamic counselling is not problem-centred (in other words it does not concentrate upon presenting problems), the types of problem which people present, and their ways of reacting to difficulties, serve as guides to understanding the whole person. Presenting problems, other than those expressed in the first session, can be included in this section, especially if it is possible to suggest any conflicts which may be currently related to them.

Underlying Conflicts (and Past Problems)

(a) Affection for some men (grandfather and Kit); other men as 'rotten': ambivalent feelings: splitting? Feelings as a child about her father, described as 'a sponger' by grandfather, contributing to splitting?

(b) Through grandfather's care of her has seen men as nurturing (mother-substitute). Difficulty of making transition to see them as sexual objects?

(c) Has had to act as a substitute for grandmother and mother in grandfather's eyes, and not allowed to develop in her own right?

The psychodynamic approach generally lays considerable stress upon the influence of past experience: both real events and relationships, and the feelings, thoughts and fantasies evoked by them. In short-term psychodynamic counselling it is often not possible to do much more than introduce a few references to past experience. Nevertheless, in Western society the Freudian influence has been strong, and the notion that the past affects the present is not confined to those who have read some psychoanalytic literature. Clients regularly introduce references to their past, sometimes the relatively recent past, but sometimes their childhood. There is often a wish to understand why they feel the way they do, or why relationships take a particular form. In psychodynamic counselling the client's wish to relate past and present is welcomed, as a means of understanding, and hopefully of beginning to change the present. Hannah's story in the first session included past experience, and provided me with ideas that might help her to understand both her depression and her antipathy towards men.

She spoke of her grandfather, and of Kit, in a positive way, although edged with hostility. She described in more negative terms her feelings about her father, her brother, and their recent landlord. I felt, knowing a little of her history from her as a result of the first session, that there were other, less obvious conflicts, which had arisen in the past, and still influenced her now. Her grandfather had taken over the care of Hannah when her mother had died, and perhaps had become for her a substitute of the mother she had lost. What had this meant for her as she grew up? His being for her both a mother and a father may have led to some confusion in Hannah's mind as to how to relate not only to him, but also to other men as her sexual feelings and conscious awareness developed. As far as counselling was concerned, Hannah wanted to see a woman, not a man, because a man roused anxieties about sexual relationships – hence her initial question about psychoanalysis. I had the feeling that it was only because I had assumed a more nurturing role in her mind as the first session developed that she was able to relate to me at all; had I presented a sexual threat to her, she would not have come back. My maleness had for the time being to be played down, although it could not go on being denied, if Hannah was to take any significant step towards resolving some of these possible conflicts.

Hannah had also been a substitute figure for her grandfather. She had probably become a substitute daughter, following her mother's early death. But since her mother in her turn might well have replaced her own mother, and therefore in some sense been a substitute wife for grandfather, it seemed possible that Hannah had always been not only a granddaughter to the old man, but a replacement daughter and wife as well. Such multiple roles are exceedingly complex to sustain. She was certainly having to care for her grandfather now, as she appeared to have done for several years, and she was unable to free herself sufficiently from him to be able to leave him and to make her own relationships.

It is difficult in counselling to explore, to substantiate or refine, and to use all such ideas. They do, however, form a background resource to the counselling which can be drawn upon and used at any time, to throw light upon the present situation, inside and outside the counselling room. These tentative hypotheses about past conflicts may seem daunting to the person learning about counselling. They draw upon a counsellor's experience of having worked with different clients, and upon knowledge of patterns of personality development, as understood by the psychodynamic schools of thought. Although in the first instance trainee counsellors need to concentrate more upon listening and responding to the client than upon such formulations about the client, one of the advantages of supervision is that it enables the more experienced supervisor to guide the beginner towards the development of psychodynamic hypotheses. This also applies to some of the ideas I suggest in the criteria for change that follow.

Criteria for Change

(a) Lifting of the depression.

(b) To relate to grandfather on a more equal level; and find her own identity, and to be able at least psychologically to leave him.

(c) To be able to express her frustration and anger to him, and to others, in appropriate ways.

(d) To grieve the loss of her mother, and all that entailed in her infancy and childhood.

(e) To relate to men more positively, in more complete relationships – to be able to be cared for, to care, and with an appropriate partner enjoy sexual intimacy.

This list is, to say the least, hopeful! It is not an agenda for counselling (see 'Focus' below), but rather a comprehensive set of aims, some of which might be met if counselling goes well. Counselling may help a significant change to take place in one area, even if there is little change in the others; or it might result in some progress taking place in each of the objectives.

These criteria assist the counsellor to evaluate a piece of work when it finishes (or, where facilities exist for research, at a set time after the termination of counselling).

The five areas listed as relevant to Hannah's progress and development through counselling were based in part on her own aim in seeking help, which was to get rid of her depression, and partly on the picture of her during the first few sessions. Hannah's motive for counselling, and the reason she accepted her doctor's suggestion of it, was obviously the most important factor. Yet to my mind her depression seemed related to other factors, which might need to change as a prerequisite of her depression lifting. I had no expectation that we would do more than touch on the last two areas in the time we had available, but I wished to set out as comprehensive a picture as I could for my own work of what might constitute a positive outcome. This would help me develop a focus; and it acted as a reminder to me that even a successful outcome in Hannah's terms (the lifting of her depression) would by no means imply that all the issues had been resolved.

Focus of Counselling

Aggressive feelings towards grandfather for his demands, for letting her down. The relationship to him, and where possible to other men. Watch for opportunities to use relationship with me to draw out her suspicion that men are only out for what they can get, particularly their demands for sex.

The focus of the counsellor's work is important, because often the time is limited, and in those circumstances some goals of the counselling are more realistic than others. The value of a focus is also recognised in short-term psychodynamic psychotherapy (Malan, 1976). Although Hannah was concerned about her depression, I wondered what focus might help us to understand it, and perhaps promote the expression of anger which often underlies depression. I thought it might be the relationship with the grandfather, although it might also be valuable to see if her anger was related to other men as well – her brother, her friend Kit, the landlord, and also myself.

The focus provides the counsellor with a guiding thread, with which to pursue particular areas, while leaving others to one side. Psychodynamic counselling is not directive, but neither is it non-directive. The client is the person who sets the agenda, by speaking about what he or she wants to. At the same time the counsellor can select certain features that appear in the client's story for reflection, comment or interpretation, and can choose to ignore, at least for the time being, other features which appear less immediately relevant. The focus can be changed, or refined, as the counselling proceeds. If, for instance, the client were to introduce a new area of difficulty which supersedes those mentioned previously, the counsellor may have little choice but to pursue it.

Family Tree

The family tree is an adaptation of a feature of recording particularly used in family therapy, called the genogram. The diagrammatic representation of the family history, which can be built up over the sessions as more information becomes available to the counsellor, often highlights features in the history which add to the counsellor's perception of the client. In this case (Figure 3.1) the number of deaths of the female members of the family appears significant. Hannah is the only surviving woman in three generations where the woman has died young, close to childbirth, and Hannah is now twenty-three years old, the same age as her grandmother when she died. This may mean that she is seen by her grandfather as at the crucial age, when he lost his wife, which might make him more clinging, and determined not to lose her too. Hannah may also feel some anxiety about her own age, wondering whether she is destined for an early death, like her mother and grandmother, or concerned on another level about marriage, because pregnancy seems, in her family's past, to have been attended by fatality. (For the use of genograms, see Burnham, 1986: Chapter 2.)

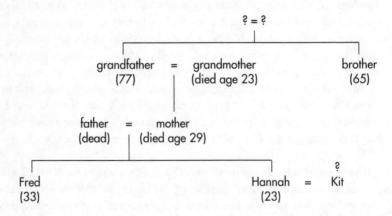

FIGURE 3.1 *Hannah's family tree*

Appearance

Slight build; pale, strained; neat, but not over-dressed, in dark colours; sad, wide open eyes, petite features, attractive, but somewhat 'china doll' facially.

Referred by

Dr Jones, after Hannah consulted her for a prescription. No medication offered. Hannah made her own appointment to see me. But did she come to please Dr Jones?

Possible Approaches

Could refer to woman counsellor; or to psychotherapy; but another referral not wise, since referral to me already seen as rejection by doctor; and seems to respond satisfactorily both to me and to counselling.

I had found Hannah hostile at first, but she had responded well to the interventions I made; and she was ready to work with me, whatever hostility she was still feeling towards men, or towards the 'Freudian' ideas she had questioned at the outset. Positive and negative feelings seemed to balance each other; and sufficient rapport developed in the first session to make referral elsewhere seem like yet another rejection. I agreed with Dr Jones that working with a man would probably be even more beneficial for Hannah than working with a woman.

Offer and Responses

To meet for three months, until mid-summer; then review. Hannah surprised by amount of time suggested: 'Does that mean I'm mad?' I said, 'Angry perhaps, not crazy.' She accepted offer, but looked a little hesitant.

I look at the 'contract' for counselling in the next chapter, where Karl's response to my offer is very different from Hannah's. It is always possible that the client who accepts a period of counselling does not in fact turn up to the second session. The particular observation in this section of the notes then enables the counsellor to see if there is any hint of a reason for absence. Hannah's hesitancy, and her fresh anxiety that the offer of counselling appeared to suggest she was mentally ill, prepared me for that eventuality although, as it turned out, she came to counselling regularly.

Outcome

[Much less depressed; able to confront her grandfather with some of her more negative feelings. Sustained a good relationship with me, in which able to voice positive as well as negative feelings; and some recognition that male sexuality need not be an expression of domination and power. Underlying grief at loss of mother, and her own emerging fear of death remained largely untouched, but could form basis for psychotherapy when she resettles. The restlessness, which meant counselling had to finish early, possibly also symptomatic of the deeper search for mother, and the inability to break free of grandfather.]

I put the final heading in parenthesis, in order to complete the picture of notes on a client, although this section would not be completed until counselling had ended. By referring to the 'Criteria for Change' listed earlier, I was able to assess how far Hannah had come in the ten sessions we had together.

THEMES IN THE SESSIONS

With factual material recorded on one record sheet, and the various headings which serve as guides to a psychodynamic understanding of the material on another, it is possible to make notes on the actual sessions in more thematic ways, including the main areas which arise, and the counsellor's interventions in response to them. Hannah's first session was summarised as shown in Figure 3.2.

The session is recorded by sketching in the main themes, and the principal interventions by the counsellor, together with the direction his or her remarks took the client. At the head of the session record is noted any change reported by the client, or seen in the session by the counsellor. This can therefore include feelings and appearance: Hannah came to her second session wearing rather brighter colours. Also recorded is the way in which the counsellor perceived his or her own manner, and 'counter-transference' feelings: feelings and thoughts evoked in the counsellor by the client. I explain this concept, and its practical use, in Chapter 6. The heading 'Missed', at the head of the session, is used to record dates where the

Session: 1	Date: 10.4.87	Missed: –

Client	Counsellor
Changes/manner	**Manner/counter-transference**
Hostile at first, then upset. Talked more freely, some hesitancy at end about leaving room	*At first felt under attack. Then concern, and gentle, comforting feelings. Wary*

Themes	Interventions
Query about psychoanalysis	*Afraid I'll be interested in sex?*
Implied wish to go on seeing her doctor (woman)	*Lacks sense of her value?*
Looking after others – see factual material (grandfather)	*(Listened, prompted)*
Leaving London – see factual material	*(Asked some questions.) Sounds like a big loss*
My remark led her to speak of other losses in her family (see factual material)	*Difficult to trust anyone – feeling that those you trust only let you down*
She agreed with my remark	*Arranged meetings ahead*

Afterthoughts
Perhaps her hesitancy about seeing me is because she thinks I will let her down like others – caring inevitably leads to disappointment? I missed seeing that possible link.

FIGURE 3.2 *Summary of Hannah's first session*

client cancels or does not appear, or when there is a planned break. I also record there if I write a letter to the client following a missed appointment, which I may do if I have particular cause for concern. At the foot of the session the section called 'Afterthoughts' is space for any ideas which occur to the counsellor while writing up the session, or as a result of supervision, as well as any thoughts which occurred during the session but which were not then expressed, either because they were only half formed, or because it would have been inappropriate to have voiced them at that point.

MAKING AN ASSESSMENT

A system of recording the main features in the client's case-history has a further advantage, since it provides the psychodynamic counsellor with relevant information with which to assess the appropriateness for the client of this particular method of counselling. During the first session (although sometimes it may take a further meeting to clarify doubtful factors), the counsellor needs to make a decision, whether what he or she can offer, both in terms of time and of expertise, is going to be of value to the client. While the client is the one who makes the final decision to accept or refuse an offer of further counselling, the responsible counsellor does not offer the false promise of help when he or she feels little hope of success.

In assessing, a counsellor is not looking simply at what the client is like now, but at her or his potentiality for using counselling. If it seems that a client can be helped, early in counselling, to shift from unrealistic expectations of the counsellor to a more active involvement in the process, the client may indeed find counselling helpful. Such fine distinctions are present in every assessment, and make all the difference between offering more time to clients, or referring them elsewhere.

The question of assessment is complicated by the lack of any hard-and-fast distinction between counselling and psychotherapy. Each end of the spectrum may be clear: where there is a short series of sessions dealing with a current issue alone, in which the counsellor's interventions are mainly reflective, assisting the client in working on his own feelings and solutions, we recognise counselling. Where there are twice-weekly sessions, which have gone on for two years, working on the influence of the past on the present, and with interpretation of the transference (explained further in Chapter 6), we recognise psychotherapy. However, there are many other instances in the middle of this continuum where the line between counselling and psychotherapy is not at all clear. Some practitioners offer both counselling and psychotherapy, some may call themselves both psychodynamic counsellor and psychodynamic psychotherapist, and some prefer one title to the other for a variety of reasons. In some instances clients may start by coming for brief counselling, but show the need and capacity for longer-term counselling or psychotherapy. I have raised elsewhere some of the difficulties of distinguishing the two terms, as well as suggested some parameters for determining difference (Jacobs, 1994).

It is possible to make various distinctions when assessing clients, as to whether or not a client is suitable for psychodynamic counselling, and if not whether the client could be referred to longer-term psychotherapy; or whether he or she might benefit from other forms of counselling or therapy, from behaviour therapy through to psychotropic medication. But I have found myself challenged over what seems now a simplistic version of which client is suitable for what, set out in the first edition of this book. What may have been true in the 1980s is no longer as clear as counselling moves into the second millennium. Counsellors are seeing clients, who some years ago would have been classified as beyond their skills and training. They have shown the capacity to work with such clients, partly because there is no one else available who can, and partly because the level of training in counselling, and their supervision, has greatly increased the wider application of counselling. Responding to the challenge, I have questioned my earlier views:

> It may be possible therefore to distinguish not between counsellors and psychotherapists, but between experienced practitioners and inexperienced or even pedestrian practitioners . . . Certain presenting problems, borderline personalities, character disorders, some survivors of abuse and trauma require an experienced counsellor or therapist. A range of subtle skills, such as understanding at an intuitive level as well as the recognition of 'not-knowing', and the ability to stay with and yet at the same time work on and work through, are more typical of the experienced practitioner.
>
> Assessment remains essential when counsellors or new therapists are allocated clients. Assessment skills are essential element in more experienced practitioners. Good supervision similarly plays a crucial role, enabling counsellors and therapists who show obvious promise to develop towards working with more problematic clients. Counselling courses where there is a high level of expertise in supervisors, or counselling agencies which draw upon experienced therapists as supervisors, can produce counsellors who are as effective as any registered psychotherapist. (Jacobs, 1996c: 6)

In listening to the client, and assessing how well the client and psychodynamic counsellor will suit each other, the counsellor has in mind many of the factors listed in Figure 3.3. In some instances these factors suggest a suitable person for psychodynamic work generally; in others, work that should only be undertaken by the experienced, skilled counsellor or therapist; and in others (obviously often the reverse of such features) the indications suggest an alternative form of help.

Suitable clients for psychodynamic counselling and therapy	Only suitable for experienced psychodynamic counsellors and therapists	Unlikely to be suitable for psychodynamic counselling or psychotherapy *
recent onset of problems (or of a new problem)	long-standing problems	seen many helpers for only short time, maybe over many years (and/or currently seeing another helper)
possible reasons for problem clear	clear difficulties but not clear reasons for them	very narrowly defined problems (monosymptomatic)
verbalises thoughts and feelings	verbalises, but tends to intellectualise feelings; may be rather passive, but is responsive	cannot express in words, or take initiative in talking; passive and unresponsive
relates, well or badly, to at least one other person	unable to form close relationships	no wish to form relationship with counsellor or therapist
trusts counsellor; can allow some dependence	over-dependent or shows deep inability to trust	unable to allow any dependency on others
tolerates once-weekly sessions	may sometimes or for a long time need to be seen more than once weekly	only wants occasional sessions
able to see own contribution to difficulties	narcissistic character, over-concern about self	only blames others
wish to understand self	wish for deeper insight than possible in short-term contract	wishes to be rid of symptoms, by 'magic'
does not act out	some acting-out but with insight into reasons for it	severe acting-out of problems – no insight into reasons for it
desire for change, and problems ego-dystonic	desire for change, although some problems may be ego-syntonic	no desire for change
normally well-functioning central ego	weak central ego but able to use therapist to support ego strength	dependent on high dosage of drugs, even if medically prescribed
able to tolerate disturbing feelings and thoughts; central self feels in sufficient control	bizarre and disturbing thoughts and behaviour but able to recognise this and can manage life day by day	bizarre and disturbing thoughts and behaviour, which take over person's normal functioning

* unless accompanied by other therapeutic methods, or by therapists who are very experienced at handling and working with these presenting behaviours.

FIGURE 3.3 *Distinguishing features of suitable clients*

From this summary it is possible to identify some key factors:

1.   The duration of the difficulty or problem presented is relevant. If the problems are recent, and there appears to be evidence of possible reasons for the difficulties, this points towards the suitability of counselling. If, however, the problems presented have been troubling the person for many years, longer term counselling or psychotherapy is to be recommended, where the experienced practitioner is able to work through long-term problems. Having made this distinction, however, some people with long-term problems come for counselling with a different, more immediate problem of another kind; or are in the midst of a short-term situation which makes their long-term difficulties more difficult to bear than usual. Briefer counselling might be helpful for a period, although it will, in such instances, often be of a supportive kind, with interpretations kept to a minimum, and with encouragement given for every positive move which the client shows signs of making. I do not believe that brief counselling is any easier than long-term work, and indeed it could be argued that brief work requires sufficient experience to be able to see quickly to the heart of issues. But some supportive work from caring and enthusiastic 'beginners' can sometimes prove effective, at least in the immediate crisis.

If the difficulties have extended over many years, or the assessor cannot see any clear (possible) reasons for more acute problems, he or she may consider referring the client to a very experienced counsellor or therapist. Whether it is counselling or psychotherapy which is considered, the question of duration of problems is only one issue; the features which follow also apply, so that, for instance, even short-term difficulties with an obvious cause will not be amenable to counselling if the client does not want to talk!

2.   An important part of counselling is the opportunity to express feelings and thoughts. This means that a client needs to use her or his own words to communicate what he or she is thinking or feeling, as well as to be in touch with more obvious feelings and thoughts. The silent person, who can only answer 'yes' or 'no', or who does not speak without first being asked a question, is unlikely to make use of a method which depends upon the client taking the initiative, and which asks the client to speak freely about anything and everything that comes to mind.

It is important, however, to distinguish between the type of people who lack social skills, and who are so passive that they cannot speak until spoken to, and clients who are temporarily withdrawn and silent, perhaps through shock or deep depression, but who until recently have been more active in their communication with others. Some enquiry about how the person felt *before* the onset of present problems helps the counsellor to assess the permanent or temporary nature of the silent client.

Some clients speak freely, but show little capacity to reflect upon themselves; or they intellectualise their experience rather than show any real feeling about it. Talking can become defensive, a way of warding off painful insight or feeling. A more experienced counsellor is likely to be of more help in such instances, unless the problem happens to be one which can be resolved just by thinking about it, in which case a cognitive approach might be better than a psychodynamic approach. Where there are clear resistances to be overcome (see Chapter 5), the experienced practitioner is more appropriate, especially if these defences serve to keep other people in their lives at a distance.

3. This brings out a third feature which helps distinguish the client who is more suitable for the experienced and skilled counsellor and therapist than for the beginner: the man or woman who appears to have made no close relationships with others, whose history may reflect lack of a relationship of any depth, and yet one who seeks and wants help. The emotionally cut-off or withdrawn person is technically known as 'schizoid'. This is not to be confused with schizophrenic, which is by contrast a bizarre state. The schizoid person may in many respects seem quite ordinary. Psychodynamic psychotherapy has given much attention to the schizoid character. A shorter-term contract can sometimes help the schizoid person who seeks help for some other problem, to move into long-term counselling or psychotherapy.

In psychodynamic counselling it is important that the client should have or have had at least one close relationship. It does not matter if such a close relationship has or had considerable negative feelings in it as well as positive ones, but the psychodynamic counsellor looks for some sign that the client shows the capacity to relate to others. This augurs well for a relationship with the counsellor too. A person who seems only to argue with his partner is thus more suitable for counselling than a person who appears *unable to relate at all* to his partner, and for the latter very experienced psychotherapists and counsellors would be essential.

4. The relationship between the counsellor and client includes a tacit agreement to work together. For this working alliance to function satisfactorily, the assessment of the client aims to distinguish whether the client shows the ability to trust the counsellor, and the capacity to place some reliance upon the counsellor's skills and expertise. The person who is unable to trust, and is fiercely independent, is unlikely to stay in

counselling for long. At the same time, counselling requires a client to cope with the week between sessions without recourse to the counsellor. The suitable client either has other supportive relationships, or can tolerate painful feelings without needing extra time. Where a client is likely to become more dependent upon the helper, then greater experience is necessary in the counsellor or therapist. It may be necessary to meet more than once a week (usually only offered by psychotherapists), or a therapeutic community – where there is constant professional help – may be more suitable.

Likewise, psychodynamic counselling and psychotherapy are not generally suitable for clients who persist in seeking magical answers from their counsellor, or from anyone else. In counselling and in psychotherapy, the client has to tolerate the frustration of symptoms not being relieved in a short time, and of not finding immediate answers to pressing personal questions. The client needs to show some capacity to enter counselling as a partner, working with the counsellor, making her or his own contributions to understanding. The wish to understand is of particular importance in psychodynamic therapy and counselling, where insight is felt to be an important factor in promoting change.

Of course, clients who are suitable do not necessarily show the features mentioned here at the first interview. They may have no knowledge of counselling, and may come expecting something to be done for them or to them. What is important is that such clients show the ability to accept changes in their expectations, and to respond to the responsibility which the counsellor or therapist tries to share with them.

5.   Furthermore, clients who are suitable for psychodynamic counselling and psychotherapy need to develop the capacity to see their own contribution to their difficulties, so that they do not lay the responsibility for their troubles solely on other people or upon external circumstances. In assessment, a counsellor looks for evidence of such insight, aware that counselling and therapy cannot change external circumstances or other people; it can only assist change in the client, who may then be able to take steps to alter external circumstances, or to improve other relationships. Connected with this feature is the ability of suitable clients to identify with the feelings of others, and to see how they affect and are affected by other people. Such ability is probably more necessary in counselling, where time is limited, than in long-term counselling or psychotherapy. In the latter, the narcissistic character (someone who seems only to be able to think of her or his own feelings and interests) has a greater opportunity to work through their own deep-seated needs, and

so be able to build up a sufficient sense of self to be able to feel and show concern for others.

6. Although the wish to change may initially appear to be a very obvious requirement of a client, it is important for counselling and psychotherapy that presenting symptoms and other difficulties are sufficiently disturbing and uncomfortable for the client to want to be free of them. Technically, symptoms can be described as 'ego-dystonic' (out of tune with the person) or 'ego-syntonic' (in tune with the person). If the symptoms provide too much reward and pleasure for the client, he or she is unlikely to want to give them up. For instance, it may be difficult to give up a pattern of behaviour, even though it causes distress to self or others, until the point when it either impinges painfully upon the self or threatens to damage relationships, or gives rise to other difficulties which have the same effect.

Good motivation does not in itself prevent resistance to change, because some attitudes and patterns of behaviour are not lightly given up. These patterns often serve a purpose, giving expression to one repressed part of the person that needs to make its voice heard. This means that counselling in particular requires a client with a central, observing and experiencing ego, that is strong enough to want to understand the other aspects of the self, and which is prepared to give those aspects a voice, while at the same time not letting them take control. If the client's ego is weak, and readily succumbs to the pressures either of impulses or strong feelings, or to the punishing voice of the super-ego or conscience, more experienced counsellors and therapists tend to have a more confident sense of getting the balance right between containing and challenging, between supportive and insight-oriented work.

One aspect of the client's wish to change might be seen through the route by which the client has come for counselling. If the client has been sent by someone else, or comes only because of threats on the part of others (such as a partner or an authority figure), the psychodynamic counsellor has to test the client's own motivation, and work with the client so that he or she makes his or her own choice whether or not to continue.

THE UNSUITABLE CLIENT

There are certain clear contra-indications for counselling in general, which also apply to psychodynamic counselling, in addition to the negative features explained in the preceding section. Where any of these appear, counselling is likely to be of limited value, except perhaps as a way of guiding a person to more appropriate channels to help.

1.   The client who has seen many helpers and counsellors before, and stayed only a short time with each of them, is likely to do the same in psychodynamic counselling.

2.   If the client is currently seeing another counsellor or therapist, or someone who offers a similar type of help, then the psychodynamic counsellor can only go as far as exploring with the client what seems not to be working in the help presently being received; and encouraging the client to see just one therapist.

3.   The client who shows previous or present evidence of particular forms of 'acting out' is not a good prospect for counselling. 'Acting out' is a technical psychoanalytic term which describes people who act damagingly towards themselves and/or others outside the counselling session, and are unable to confine themselves to expressing feelings in words, both in counselling and outside it. Acting out can take many forms, including potentially dangerous actions, such as addictions and substance abuse, violence towards self or others, inappropriate and promiscuous sexual relationships, uncontrollable behaviour, and even compulsive rituals. Although experienced therapists and counsellors may be able to contain such behaviour, and help its modification through management and interpretative work, in extreme cases much more directive forms of therapy may be necessary.

4.   Another contra-indication is where a single, narrowly defined problem is presented, without there appearing to be anything else amiss in the client's life; for example, a single phobia, or a psychosomatic symptom, apparently unconnected with anything else. Some clients who present one issue soon show themselves willing to extend their thinking to other aspects of themselves, and when this happens psychodynamic counselling can turn attention towards, for example, the client's relationships rather than the initial presenting symptoms. Nevertheless, a client who continues to be obsessed with the initial presenting problem is unlikely to benefit from the psychodynamic approach.

5.   The client who is on a high continual dosage of medication is rarely suitable for psychodynamic counselling or therapy, unless the counsellor is able to work with the prescribing doctor or psychiatrist to reduce the medication, which may happen as the counselling relationship becomes more significant for the client. Even then, it is counselling or psychotherapy with the experienced practitioner that is likely to be more appropriate if, like the use of medication, the client's difficulties go back over years.

6.   Liaison with the medical profession is an important part of a counsellor's work, although the issue of confidentiality requires that a
counsellor seeks the client's permission before talking with a doctor, or
indeed with anyone else in the client's life. If a client presents a combination of physical and emotional symptoms, a counsellor needs to check
that the client is under medical care, and that the doctor is aware that his
or her patient has come for counselling. It is irresponsible to offer counselling for emotional problems, where there is any possibility that they
may be connected with physical or organic illness, without first having
these checked out (e.g. head pains or impotence).

7.   Finally, the list of those unsuitable for counselling includes people
whose thought patterns are very disturbed, whose behaviour is bizarre,
whose ideas seem totally irrational, without their realising it, who seriously fear losing control, and those whose conversation flits from subject
to subject without any obvious connections ('a butterfly-mind'), and those
who arouse in the counsellor real concern for their sanity. The function of
the counsellor is to listen to such clients sensitively and for sufficiently
long to help steer them towards medical, psychiatric or psychological
help. Referral (see below) is a specially delicate skill, especially when such
persons claim bad experiences with, and hence suspicion of, doctors and
hospitals.

ASSESSING KARL

Karl did not immediately appear a very good prospect for counselling,
whether or not it was psychodynamic in orientation. In my estimation he
had begun the first session somewhat ominously, with references to having
seen many people before me, including an astrologer, with whom I had no
particular wish to be bracketed. He had also started by idealising me.
There were hints of paranoid thoughts. He changed subjects rather rapidly, showing signs of that butterfly-type thinking of which the counsellor
needs to be cautious. He appeared to have a very magical idea of what
counselling might achieve, both through me reading his mind, and also by
me being the one who was to sort him out. Despite his attempts at flattery
early on, there did not seem a lot of rapport between us, since I did not
feel comfortable in his presence, and he did not appear to be responding
to much of what I had said.

Nevertheless, as he continued in the first session, I found that by letting
him wander around there seemed more sense in what he was saying than

at first appeared. When he had talked of feeling robbed, I had imagined some paranoid fantasy. He did not make the connection himself, but I certainly felt he had been robbed when he went on to tell me that he was a naturalised citizen, who had previously lived in Eastern Europe. There he had been gaoled for his political views, and while in prison his wife had left him for another man. (He had been robbed not only of freedom, but also of his wife.) Their daughter had been taken in by relatives, and when he had been released, following a relaxation of the hardened attitudes of the state, he had been allowed to leave the country, taking her with him.

In telling me this, Karl both elicited more sympathy from me, and also provided me with a much richer picture of the last ten years. That he should have appeared paranoid now seemed to have some reality factors. The years in prison had left their mark upon him, and I was unhappy at the degree of damage which such an experience might have wrought upon him. I was unsure whether counselling was going to be able to give him as much help as he hoped for. It was still not clear from the first session why he had come to see me at this point in time, or indeed whether anything in particular had been troubling him when he had gone to see the astrologer.

He had been a professional man in his own country, and had found it difficult to get into the same profession in his country of adoption. An English friend, whom I had met socially, had recommended he come to see me, but again Karl gave no real reason for this suggestion. It was difficult to see what current conflicts there were, apart from the realistic ones of settling into a different culture, and trying to find work. His past difficulties were much clearer, because of all the feelings that he was left with, as a result of the experience of being a political prisoner.

On the negative side, therefore, Karl was unsuitable for counselling because his current problems seemed too wide-ranging, and yet also imprecise, with no clear trigger for his seeking help at this point in time. He had seen other helpers before, but only for a short time. He seemed to expect me to make things better for him. He appeared distracted, not always in contact with me. More positively, he spoke fairly freely, without needing any prompting from me; he appeared to be coming of his own volition; and he had described experiences which seemed to justify any strangeness there might be about him.

I felt that he had many adjustments to make, and that counselling could provide some support for him during the next few months. At the same time my initial anxiety about him had not totally disappeared, and I thought that in my own interventions I should try to avoid saying anything too challenging. My main role was to support him in making any changes which he might want to make and which seemed positive for him to effect. I thought it might also help him talk about the deprivations resulting from his imprisonment, which, as the next chapter shows, was not easy for him to do.

As it turned out my initial anxieties were not altogether unfounded, and my first offer was rejected. Karl's experiences had disturbed him to a far greater extent than I was able to appreciate when I began to feel sympathy for him. My difficulty empathising with his past situation was reflected in my overlooking just how devastated he had been. Although I had spotted his flattery of me, telling me of people who said I was 'good' at my job, I had nevertheless been seduced by it, mistakenly drawn into thinking he would value the offer of counselling which I made. I return to this in the next chapter.

SUPERVISION

Had I taken the first session with Karl to supervision, I might not have agreed to take him on, although some of the difficulties that arose in counselling him will serve as useful illustrations of the psychodynamic concepts which this and later chapters explain.

Psychodynamic counselling, in common with many other orientations, recognises the value, and indeed the necessity, of supervision of the counsellor. The psychodynamic approach requires a supervisor who is at least as familiar and experienced in the same method of working and understanding as the counsellor, with whom the latter can regularly meet to discuss case-work.

Supervision is conducted in a similar way to counselling itself, with the counsellor having the responsibility of bringing the client material which he or she wishes, choosing perhaps to talk about the content of a series of sessions with one client, or the particular problem areas which have arisen with one or more clients. The supervisor uses many of the skills and concepts which are described in this book, such as his or her own associations to the description of the client, feelings which he or she perceives in the counsellor in relation to the client, and interpretations which are aimed at trying to understand both the client and the counsellor – client interaction. The supervisor may also take particular notice of the relationship between supervisee and supervisor, as a possible reflection in some of its aspects of the relationship between the counsellor and the client. This is known as 'parallel process', a psychodynamic concept that seems to have found considerable favour in other types of therapy. I have some reservations about the degree to which this concept is applied, and have questioned whether there are other explanations for what appears to be a similar set of circumstances in both supervision and the therapeutic session (Jacobs, 1996b).

Part of the value of a supervisor is that, while remaining sensitive to the level of understanding on the part of the counsellor, he or she has more distance from the counselling or therapy to be able to see other dimensions (Searles, 1955). In supervision there is also greater freedom to express tentative ideas and hunches, which in counselling itself are better held back until the opportunity arises to use them. A good supervisor encourages the counsellor to join in the work of formulating hypotheses about the client.

REFERRAL BY THE COUNSELLOR

Hannah and Karl had both been referred to me, the one by her doctor, and the other more informally by Karl's professional acquaintance. I described referrals *to* a counsellor in the last chapter. Yet the assessment of a client can lead the counsellor to decide that psychodynamic counselling, or any other form of counselling, is not the appropriate help to offer, so that referral *by* the counsellor to someone else becomes necessary.

There are two aspects to referral by the counsellor which need to be considered. The first is knowing what other resources are available, and what those resources are able to provide by way of help. The psychodynamic approach is one of many, and it is useful for counsellors to know, at least in outline, what other agencies or individuals can offer, as well as what other therapeutic approaches might be able to achieve. Medical and psychiatric resources, counsellors of different orientation, therapists of different persuasions, as well as statutory and voluntary groups, can all provide alternative ways of helping. Clearly a counsellor needs to make a wise referral, one where there is a realistic chance that help can be offered. Otherwise the client could easily be passed from person to person, or from agency to agency.

Yet the client has initially come to the counsellor believing that he or she will be able to help, perhaps not knowing of other avenues, and even being reluctant to contemplate starting the whole process over again. Indeed, some clients, particularly those who are most disturbed, may resist referral to any source of help which appears to label them as psychiatrically or mentally ill. It may be necessary to ensure that sufficient trust is built up between counsellor and client for such a suggestion, delicately made, to be seen as an offer of help and not as a threat or a rejection. Although I agreed with Hannah's doctor that I might be able to help her, so that referral elsewhere was not necessary (I had some doubts that she would accept longer-term psychotherapy at this point in time), I could have considered referring Karl to someone who could assess his mental stability more accurately than I felt capable of myself. The thought crossed my mind, but I was also conscious of the way in which psychiatric hospitals had been misused in his own country (as indeed, for rather different motives, they have been in the West). I did not wish to revive the feelings of terror that he had probably experienced in his previous incarceration; and I was aware of the expression that had passed over him when he had told me about feeling 'trapped' by the astrologer's remark. Had I suggested, at least at that point, the value of some psychiatric help, I think he would have broken off all contact with me.

Other clients, who are less disturbed, but nonetheless are not suitable for psychodynamic counselling, can feel disappointment and rejection when the counsellor suggests an alternative form of therapy or help. If such feelings can be explored and voiced in the assessment interview, they are less likely to be carried over into the subsequent helping situation. The same care that the psychodynamic counsellor pays to clients who are accepted for counselling needs also to be given to the referral of those who are not. Issues around boundaries and endings may be relevant in these instances: endings I look at in Chapter 7; boundaries in the next.

4

THE IMPORTANCE OF
TIME AND BOUNDARIES

HANNAH

'Well, it's a long story, I don't know if I've got time . . .'

'We do have another forty minutes, and I think for my part that it might be helpful to meet again . . .' It was at this point that I left the verbatim record of the first session with Hannah (p. 42), and in the last chapter continued her story by reproducing the notes made after the first session. In those notes I summarised the story she had told me, as well as my own thinking about its possible meanings. The summary simply consists of the main material and ideas, and sketches the order of the first session (set out on p. 63). There are other aspects in that record, particularly the references to time and the arrangements for meeting agreed between us, which need further explanation.

The client's use of, and response to, the boundaries of time, both with respect to individual sessions and to a series of sessions, is of major significance in the psychodynamic approach. The psychodynamic theory of human development attaches considerable importance to the way in which past events influence present circumstances. Responses to others in adult life are influenced by reactions experienced by infants and children to time and space boundaries, such as periods of waiting for mother or father to come when the child needs attention. Hannah suggested her own anxieties about time early in the first session, when she commented that her doctor did not have time to see her, and when she wondered, a little later (as above), whether she would have enough time with me. I made it clear to her what time was left to her in that first session, and that it need not be the only time we met. I had, in psychodynamic terms, set out some boundaries for her. This was partly to reassure her that there was time for her to begin her long story, but it was also to introduce to her the fact that the session had to come to an end. When clients know what time limits exist in their counselling, they respond to them in different, and often significant ways.

THE PATTERN OF THE COUNSELLING SESSION

Any counselling session (and Hannah's first session illustrates this) has a pattern, of which the psychodynamic counsellor is always conscious. There is, very obvious though it may seem, a beginning, a middle and an end. The beginning of Hannah's session consisted of her expressing her reservations about seeing me. I had to show in my responses that I was a person in whom she might be able to have sufficient initial trust, for us to begin to work together.

After about ten minutes, the session moved (almost imperceptibly) into what was clearly a different theme, and a different mood. The mood was one of increased openness, the theme was Hannah's immediate circumstances, and included some information about her family background. This part of the session can be called the central section: central in time, since it forms the greatest part of the fifty minutes available to her, and central inasmuch as Hannah told me quite a lot about herself, and began to work with me on what had brought her to counselling. During this central time I was content to listen and respond in appropriate ways in order to encourage her to expand upon her story; but I also used, as explained in Chapter 2, one or two interpretative comments, to see if Hannah was likely to be a suitable person for my own approach, the psychodynamic one.

Even though Hannah had the freedom to say what she wanted, I too was conscious that in the time available I wanted to test her capacity to work with the types of link which so characterise the psychodynamic approach. I too had an agenda, related to my task of counselling, and to my wish to carry out that task effectively; and at certain points I used the openings she gave me for responding to her as a way of testing out ideas that I had in my own mind. To give another example, I was wondering in the first session with Karl, as explained in the last chapter, whether he was suitable for the type of counselling I could offer, and whether he would benefit from the relatively short time I could offer him. Some of my questions and interventions were designed to glean the information I needed for such a decision. Only after I had made my own decision could I then give Karl the opportunity of making his own choice as to whether he wished to go on seeing me or not.

There is, at least in theory, a significant difference here between the person-centred approach and the psychodynamic one. A psychodynamic counsellor has his or her own ideas, drawn from seeing other clients, to which he or she pays attention, as well as listening carefully to the client's words and feelings. While the psychodynamic counsellor accepts the individuality and uniqueness of every person (and in doing so shares the same outlook as the person-centred approach), he or she also offers more general experience and knowledge, adapted to the particular client, for the client to accept, refine or reject as the client wishes. The psychodynamic approach means that the counsellor listens not only to the client, but also to his or her learning about people, and therefore to those ideas or constructions of the client's material which come to mind. When it seems appropriate, the counsellor suggests ideas, and tests them out with the client to see if they make sense. The timing of such interventions is a skill in itself. Merely to blurt out an idea as soon as it occurs to the counsellor is to risk being completely wrong, or to risk making suggestions which the client accepts or rejects without thinking about them. It can be very invasive. A good sense of timing means that the counsellor waits upon an idea, looks for confirmation, or for evidence which helps substantiate the point; the counsellor then suggests an idea when it is at least partially developed in the client material, and when the client is perhaps on the verge of saying something similar. Although it might be said that the best-timed interventions are those which give substance to the client's own developing sense of insight, and highlight understanding which is already close to consciousness, the most satisfying are when the client says first what the counsellor was just about to try out with the client. Samuels (1985) refers to some research into counter-transference by some German analytical psychologists. They summed up their findings by the exclamation of one of their group that 'The patients continually say what I am thinking and feeling at the moment.'

In the central section of a counselling session, therefore, a psychodynamic counsellor needs first to listen carefully to what the client is expressing; as the session develops, the client's story or particular phrases may register vague ideas in the counsellor's mind; as the time progresses, in some sessions (though by no means all) words and phrases and ideas begin to form a pattern, which can then be suggested to the client. These are put to the client only if there is enough time left to check the validity of the interpretation, and sufficient time for the client to develop anything which has made sense. On occasion (and this is particularly true when first starting to practise counselling) the counsellor sees the patterns more clearly after the session, or in supervision, and has to wait for subsequent sessions to introduce an idea, if it once more appears.

The central part of the session has its own structure. The client is encouraged to take the initiative, while at first the counsellor prompts and reflects, even though the latter is at the same time engaged inwardly on the task of trying to make sense of the material. When (and if) the counsellor feels that the client has said enough to justify an interpretation, the counsellor can then introduce, in a simple, reasoned and concise form, the idea that the counsellor has in mind, and which (if the counsellor is accurate) will already be partially formed in the client's mind. This should be done when there is still sufficient time left in the session (fifteen to twenty minutes) for the client to make an adequate response, which might be to reject the idea, or might be to accept it and develop it for himself. In the remaining part of the central section of the session, the client is encouraged to work upon that interpretation, to refine it, to draw out its relevance, and to express any feelings which emerge as a result of it. Then the counsellor ensures the client moves into the end part of the session.

During the last few minutes the counsellor may need to take the initiative, particularly if the client is distressed, or is deep into working on self-understanding. In early sessions, this often involves a reminder of the amount of time left; but at any time the counsellor may deliberately have to steer the client away from upsetting thoughts or feelings, in order to help the client to leave in a stable state (at least in outward appearance). Clients often have to return to work or to resume other relationships within a few minutes. Sometimes, particularly if it appears difficult for the client to stop, the last part of the session involves looking at the feelings about having to end at such a difficult or crucial point. A client may feel (and need to be helped to say) that the counsellor seems uncaring by not giving extra time. An example of this (in Hannah's second session) appears below.

Every part of a session therefore has its own significance. The beginning, for instance, often provides a clue to the main theme or feelings that are to follow. This is why it is so important for the counsellor to let the client have the first word, because what may appear to be trivial, common-place comments by the client sometimes suggest thoughts and feelings which are already present in them. What makes a person choose a particular opening, from the many ways they could start? What is it about the particular moments of the last week which the client chooses to speak about, that marks them out from all the other hours that have passed since the last session? The psychodynamic counsellor looks at these opening minutes, and the story that the client has to tell with particular interest, to see what the client may also be saying about the here-and-now relationship between client and counsellor. Hannah, for instance, started her second session by saying, quite casually, 'I didn't think I'd get here on time. It's so annoying having to wait for buses.' I made a mental note, as I always try to do, of this remark, wondering what it meant. I had to wait for the end of the session to see what she might have meant, because when I then reminded her that we would soon have to stop, she said in reply, with a shallow sigh, 'It'll have to wait till next week then?' I said, 'I guess that's like having to wait for buses, pretty annoying.' I thought later, writing up the session, that both beginning and end were examples of the frustration she experienced generally at being 'pushed around' by men. More specifically, and being conscious that the offer of time was an important issue for Hannah, I thought that my being the one who had had to end each session to date had also made her feel she was being 'pushed around'; and perhaps annoyed at having to wait to go on with her story.

MAKING CONTRACTS

There is another aspect to time which is important to the psychodynamic counsellor (but also important to the client). This is the actual time allocated to each session, and the total time available for counselling, extending as it may over a number of weeks or months. Most psychodynamic counselling consists of once-weekly sessions, each session lasting between forty-five minutes and an hour – the 'fifty-minute hour' (an anomalous term!) is the psychoanalytic norm which has been adopted by many psychodynamic counsellors. The total number of counselling sessions is normally much less than in psychoanalytic psychotherapy. It is not unusual to make a clear contract with a new client, in which the number of sessions, or a finishing date in the future, is agreed. On occasion, particularly if client or counsellor has some doubt about the usefulness of counselling, a few initial sessions can be arranged, with the possibility of a review of the arrangement at the start of the last arranged session.

Psychotherapists and counsellors may take on a client with an 'open-ended' contract, that is, with no fixed time agreed for termination, although it may be generally understood to be, for example, a year or two years in all. But even in this latter case, when termination is eventually considered, it is planned at least a few weeks ahead (or in more extensive work, a few months ahead). A psychodynamic counsellor is concerned, on the one hand, to avoid any anxiety on the part of the client about counselling ending suddenly (which to the client might then feel like rejection for something he or she has or has not said or done); and, on the other hand, is concerned to avoid a situation where a client, perhaps because he or she is angry with the counsellor, breaks off counselling suddenly without working through the ending of counselling (see Chapter 7).

This contract is not a signed or binding agreement, although it is beginning to become clear that a written set of guidelines about the terms upon which counselling or therapy is offered is essential, to clarify arrangements for cancellations, breaks, or contacting the counsellor between sessions. It is therefore a very important part of the working alliance (see Chapter 6) between the counsellor and the client. While the contract is mainly for the benefit of the counselling itself, it is also often a necessary part of the organisation of a counsellor's timetable. The contract may be important for a counsellor so as to plan the allocation of the sessions he or she offers, so that they are fully utilised. The counselling of any one individual takes place in a setting where other individuals have to be accommodated. In a local counselling centre, for example, there are frequently waiting lists, with consequent logistical headaches for administrators. I do not want to dwell on these issues, except to observe that questions of time, information for clients, and management are part of the reality of a busy counselling practice.

The counselling contract is valuable to many clients because it sets their counselling in the context of a limited amount of time. Some people use the opportunity to meet for six to ten weeks as a chance to concentrate upon a particular issue. Others put considerable thought into the times between sessions, working hard to make sense of their experience, and using the sessions to clarify and sharpen their thinking. Some find a short and limited contract less threatening than an open-ended commitment to meet, often because they fear becoming dependent upon the counsellor. For others, the knowledge that they have a regular time allocated to them each week, for a certain period of time, acts as a lifeline which holds them while they pass through a crisis. Clients are also prepared by this setting of limits for the time when they will have to 'go it alone'.

The clarification of practical arrangements is necessary for clients, but equally important is the way in which they emotionally experience the limitations on time. If Hannah, at the end of the second session, could express some frustration at having to stop after fifty minutes, it is not hard to imagine the feelings that are aroused in many clients when they have to stop seeing the counsellor altogether. The issues connected with ending are taken up more fully in the final chapter; but it is the setting of boundaries on the duration of counselling as a whole, as well as on the time available in any one session, that enables the psychodynamic counsellor to work with the feelings that accompany loss and limitation. As I explained in the first chapter, a counsellor cannot become a substitute parent, except in very limited ways (by being reliable and caring, for example); the comparatively brief amount of time the counsellor offers the client, even in a long-term contract, underlines that fact. Because a counsellor cannot give unlimited time, nor instant sessions on demand (or request), and because counselling at some point has to stop, feelings are often re-awakened in clients that remind them of the times they felt let down by their parents or other significant people in their lives. While psychodynamic counselling encourages a certain degree of dependency, it only does so as a means of helping a person towards making more reliable inter-dependent relationships with others, rather than clinging to others or being demanding of them. Acknowledgement of the boundaries between people, such as is demonstrated in psychodynamic counselling, is important in the making of such relationships.

An Example of Making the Contract

We can see how the contract is made, and some reactions to it, in this extract from Hannah's first session. We join it as Hannah is in mid-sentence, about five minutes from the time I had in mind to stop:

'. . . and he used to just go off and leave me in the flat alone, sometimes not coming back until some unearthly hour in the early morning.'

She paused, and I interjected: 'It may seem as if I am having to leave you on your own now for a while, because we have to finish in a few minutes.' I thought afterwards that I should have asked her how she felt about stopping at that point, but I was aware of the time slipping away, and had perhaps not intervened early enough. I had waited rather too long for a moment when I might take up her own words, and relate them to the end of the session. So instead I went on: 'I said earlier that I felt it would be helpful to meet again. How do you feel about that?'

Hannah looked as if she was agreeable to this suggestion, and I continued: 'Perhaps we could make an arrangement to meet weekly until July – that's about twelve weeks in all.' I felt that we would need at least this amount of time to help her express some of her deeper feelings, and I also wanted to give her the assurance that she could have the time she had earlier appeared to want.

This may have seemed a fairly short period to me, but it clearly disturbed Hannah. There was a lot of difference between meeting a second time, and commitment to meet into the more distant future. She looked surprised, and then worried. She said nothing.

'You're not sure about that?'

'You told me you weren't a psychoanalyst . . . July? Does that mean you think there's something wrong with me? Do you think I'm mad or something?'

'No, I don't think you're mad, not in the sense you mean it, you're not crazy; though I think you're pretty angry, perhaps feeling mad at me at the moment?'

'Why should I be angry with you?'

I did not want to get drawn by that question, because I may have been mistaken, and in any case time was running out, and we still had not agreed on our arrangements. 'I think it might be helpful to meet until the middle of the summer. I have my holiday in June, and it would mean we could meet for about eight weeks before my holiday, and a few more sessions after it.' (The break in counselling might be important, but I had also now reduced my offer to more manageable proportions.)

Hannah hesitantly expressed her agreement. 'You want me to go now?'

'We do have to stop there.' Here again, I avoided answering her question directly, which could have led to complications. Had I said a straight 'Yes' it would have sounded very rejecting. Had I said 'No, but I have to stop there', I might have given a rather seductive impression (given her distrust of men) that I wanted her to stay. A counsellor's choice of words and phrases is very deliberate. The psychodynamic approach is open to the criticism that in some respects the counsellor or therapist is selective, and hence somewhat artificial. I would myself prefer to say that the psychodynamic counsellor is careful and cautious, aware that his or her words can easily be distorted and cause a wrong impression. Nevertheless, the counsellor exercises control over what he or she says, just as he or she does over the timing and frequency of the sessions. My final words to Hannah in that first session – 'we do have to stop there' – affirmed the ultimate control that I had over the time we started and finished. (I examine the issue of how the question of control shifts during a therapeutic contract in *The Presenting Past* (1998), Chapter 6.)

Maintaining boundaries

Maintaining boundaries is a help to some clients, but it also causes frustration to others. As I explain in Chapter 6, the counselling relationship is a working partnership. This means that what the client says and thinks is just as important as what the counsellor thinks and says; but at the same time, a counsellor has his or her own ideas, and the counsellor shares these, as and when appropriate, with the client. So the working alliance involves a mutual give-and-take.

There is, similarly, withholding on both sides. No counsellor is able to give him- or herself unreservedly to one client. A counsellor therefore has to suggest the frequency and duration of their meetings to the client (although the client can, of course, negotiate or decline the offer). Most counsellors are limited as to just how much time they can offer to any one client, and this limits the counsellor's freedom to negotiate. Because the counsellor normally has greater experience of counselling than the client, it is natural too that the counsellor should suggest an initial contract, even though counsellor and client may later re-negotiate it. It is important to recognise the reality of the counsellor's position, as ultimately having more say than the client does, over how often and for how long they can meet. This arises out of practical considerations, having other clients to see and other commitments to uphold. It is, however, also because the psychodynamic counsellor regards setting clear boundaries as valuable in itself, as being containing for the client, as well as convenient for the counsellor. Likewise, it is the counsellor who has ultimate control over the length of a session, and over whether or not to give extra time or further sessions should a client make such a request.

Yet, on the other side, clients can (and do!) also withhold, and may choose to exercise their own form of control. It is the client who ultimately decides whether or not to accept the offer of counselling, and the suggested contract. It is the client who decides whether or not to attend any session; whether to come on time or to arrive late; whether to say anything or not; and the client has the choice of walking out of a session before the end, and abruptly terminating counselling altogether, in the way that no responsible counsellor ever would. I look at the significance of some of these responses to limitations of time in the example of Karl below.

A psychodynamic counsellor is aware both of giving and withholding. He or she is committed to the client, and to their agreement to meet. The counsellor is there, on time, week by week (unless unavoidably absent through illness or some other serious reason). Such reliability is no doubt the hallmark of any counsellor. In the psychodynamic approach, a counsellor tries not to start any session late, or indeed to begin earlier than the time stated – Hannah got quite irritated when I started five minutes early on one occasion because she was there waiting for me. She said she missed the time to 'unwind' after leaving work, before the session started. If there has to be any alteration to a regular arrangement, it is essential to give clients as much notice as possible. When a counsellor has prior knowledge of having to be absent, he or she should share this with the client, if possible a few weeks beforehand. Holidays (including the client's) and other breaks are also mentioned well before they happen.

All this is done in the name of constancy and reliability, so that the client knows that the counsellor will not deliberately, or even casually, let her or him down, and that if the counsellor has to be absent, it is not because of anything the client has said or done. Nevertheless, some clients find it difficult to believe that anyone can be reliable, and some blame themselves if, for instance, their counsellor has to cancel a session through illness, or re-arrange one for any other reason. If a counsellor can show, by adhering to arrangements, that the reality is that most people can be relied upon, and that their absence does not imply criticism or rejection of the client, some of these clients come to recognise that their present difficulties about trusting others lie currently in them more than in other people, even if at one time in the past they had very good reason to feel let down and rejected.

Though the psychodynamic counsellor gives a certain amount of time, he or she does not readily give more, unless the client's particular situation appears to warrant it. And even then, on occasions, the counsellor has to turn down requests for extra help, simply because there is literally no opportunity to meet without pushing other clients out. Other aspects of the counsellor's control over time and boundaries include the end of sessions, the counsellor's unavoidable absences, such as illness or holidays, the occasional need to change the day or times of sessions, including perhaps an occasion when the counsellor wants to make an alteration to the time, having previously been unable to meet a client's request for a change. All these examples may be occasions that give rise to strong feelings in the client, feelings which the psychodynamic counsellor is keen to draw out: feelings perhaps of anger, frustration, rejection, even of guilt for having asked for too much. Such feelings may be linked to the client's central concerns, that the counsellor has already identified as forming a focus of their work together. I did this with Hannah, who felt a similar (though less intense) frustration at my keeping her waiting a week for another session, as she did in relation to other relationships with men. If a client's reactions to the setting of boundaries are particularly intense, they are probably more closely related to earlier incidents of frustration than they are to the present situation. Such reactions can be used, as at other points in psychodynamic counselling, to help the client understand the link between past and present feelings. In Hannah's case this was especially related to people who had been, or who were, in positions of control and power over her. In the psychodynamic approach, questions that arise about the timing and boundaries of counselling are nearly always opportunities for learning, and for initiating the process of changing differing attitudes to the boundaries on other relationships.

So the psychodynamic counsellor is far from whimsical about making practical arrangements. If we are to be realistic about counsellors (of all orientations) they *are* in powerful positions *vis-à-vis* their clients, even though they try to exercise that power wisely. The psychodynamic counsellor understands over-reactions to his or her control and knowledge (such as the fantasies which many clients have of the counsellor's omnipotence and omniscience) as similar to a child's view of the power of parents. Some clients react to a counsellor as if the counsellor were a controlling parent; others as if he or she were a depriving parent; others as if the counsellor is the parent who always knows what is best. It is also helpful to see if the client's reactions to limits set in counselling shed light on the client's feelings towards current authority figures. For many clients the issues of power and control, and of giving and withholding, such as can arise in the sessions, reflect everyday relationships and daily situations.

GIVING MORE TIME

Maintaining boundaries is therefore important. Clients are secure in the knowledge that a particular time is theirs, no more but also no less. The counsellor who can maintain boundaries is also able to work more effectively, especially with clinging and demanding clients (who are not really suitable for short-term counselling, but sometimes only show their deeper problems after a few sessions). It is important for a counsellor to know that he or she has space too, and that the sometimes arduous task of listening, containing and trying to understand lasts no more than an hour at a time.

At the same time, a counsellor who knows how to maintain boundaries also needs to learn when to be more flexible, such as knowing when to extend the time if a client is deeply upset at the end of the hour, or sensing when it is appropriate to find time for an extra session, should a crisis in a client's circumstances suggest this is necessary. Such delicate decisions need to bear in mind that sometimes even a really distressed client can gain more confidence from coping on her or his own, and indeed may find new strength and hopefulness in being encouraged to struggle on until the next scheduled session. At such times it is rewarding for the counsellor to hear an otherwise rather dependent client say: 'I nearly phoned you up and asked if I could come and see you before today, but then I decided I'd try and work out what you might say if I told you what I was going through. I found that way I was able to work it out for myself.'

Clients who describe this type of inner conversation between themselves and their counsellor demonstrate how the counsellor has become 'internalised' in their inner world. In their imagination such clients can hold on to the counsellor, and look at what is happening to them through someone else's eyes as well as their own. In the development of the very young child the process of being able to internalise an image of mother is important for those periods of time when mother is not present, or is delayed in coming. At first, when a baby wakes from sleep and wants to be fed, or cleaned up, or held, the anxiety and frustration at the absence of mother soon results in crying, which becomes more and more desperate (and angry) the longer it goes on. After a few weeks, however, a baby is able to hold on to an image of mother, gurgling to her- or himself for a while, until even then the image wears thin, and physical and emotional needs prevail. As adults we too overcome having to wait for someone (a person we love) or something (a long-awaited meal) by means of internal images. Babies also use what Winnicott (1958: 229–42) calls 'transitional objects' to maintain themselves during mother's absence – objects such as a dummy, a blanket or a teddy bear, and best of all (because it cannot be dropped!) their own fist or thumb.

When clients are distressed (as may well be the case when they first come for counselling), the central ego or self is often overwhelmed by other feelings and thoughts, making it difficult for them to feel they can manage their life. A definite time to meet again can, in such instances, act as a kind of transitional object, something to hold on to until the counsellor can be seen again. The counsellor, like a mother to a baby, provides the initial strength and holding environment for the person to cope on their own between sessions. Yet some clients may find a week too long to wait, and if they appear to doubt their ability to cope, a counsellor may offer a second session within a shorter time than usual. As the client begins to 'connect' with the counsellor (that is, begins to trust the counsellor to be there, and begins to use the counsellor in imagination as someone to speak to, through inner dialogue), then such frequency of meetings often becomes less necessary. If the person is suitable for counselling (as indicated in Chapter 3), then once-weekly meetings can be arranged straightaway or within a short time. If the client needs to go on meeting more frequently than once a week, psychotherapy or counselling with a more experienced practitioner is the treatment of choice.

Once counselling has started, and the relationship has been forged sufficiently strongly for once-weekly meetings to become the norm, there may be occasions when clients appear to become particularly distressed at having to wait a whole week to see the counsellor. These may arise from particular external circumstances suddenly becoming more difficult; but they are also, in psychodynamic opinion, often linked to the way in which the client perceives the relationship he or she has with the counsellor. If for some reason the client feels that the relationship has become disconnected, then he or she may ask for an extra session or for more time. Such reasons can include the client becoming angry with the counsellor in the session (whether openly expressed or not), and yet feeling guilty about this after the session is over. An extra meeting is therefore felt to be necessary to repair the damage quickly that the client feels has been done to their relationship. Another reason could be that the counsellor said something which was less carefully considered than usual, and has offended or worried the client, so that the client feels the relationship has become strained or broken and needs to meet an extra time in order to test out whether the counsellor is still trustworthy. The counsellor can also be perceived as letting the client down by being absent (such as on holiday), or even by raising the subject of a break; anxiety at having to cope alone might become more intense in the client, perhaps compounded with feelings that the counsellor's absence is to some extent breaking trust.

When there is therefore a request for extra time by the client, or perhaps a telephone call to speak to the counsellor between sessions, it is always useful for the counsellor to think what he or she, or the client, might have said or done which could possibly have temporarily damaged, or be felt to have damaged the relationship between them. Talking this through on the telephone is sometimes sufficient in itself, although if it is really necessary (and possible) counsellor and client may have to meet for an extra session. In that case, whatever external circumstances and reasons the client gives for requesting more time, the counsellor is wise also to look at their own relationship, and especially at what might have happened in their last session to put it under strain.

Sometimes the counsellor has to take a holiday or break when the client is not yet sufficiently 'connected' to go without counselling for a few weeks. In such instances it may be necessary to arrange emergency cover (someone the client can speak to, though not for a counselling session as such); or it can be helpful to suggest the client writes down her or his experiences, in a letter or diary, which need not be sent to the counsellor (and which in any case cannot be answered) since this might encourage the process of internalisation of the counselling relationship.

Similarly, once a counselling contract has finished, a counsellor hopes that the client has sufficiently internalised the whole counselling process for the client to be able to continue self-exploration and understanding using her or his own ego-strength, and through normal relationships with others, having learned from the counsellor's attitudes and manner of working. Should the client get in contact with the counsellor, and request an extra appointment, there is no reason why an occasional session cannot be given if the counsellor has the space to do this. If, however, the request for an occasional session becomes regular, a psychodynamic counsellor again looks for what might have gone wrong in the relationship between counsellor and client, that might have led to the inability of the client to make a proper break. Sometimes feelings about the ending (see Chapter 7) have not been sufficiently expressed for the client to feel comfortable at letting the counsellor go.

CLIENT REACTIONS TO TIME

While a counsellor respects the right of a client to use, as he or she chooses, the times they have arranged together, the psychodynamic approach requires the counsellor to try to understand the misuse of time, such as coming late to sessions, wanting to leave early, or the wish to break off a contract sooner than originally agreed. Any of these circumstances might be signs of resistance, on a par with the client's choosing (consciously or unconsciously) to avoid particular subjects or to suppress certain feelings in the course of a session. This last area is examined more closely in the next chapter; here I look at the way in which time also demonstrates the possibility of resistance. Although the most obvious explanation of a client's lateness, missing a session, or terminating a contract prematurely is the one which the client gives (for example, 'the bus was late', 'I have to work a longer day next week', or 'I'm feeling so much better, I don't think we need meet anymore'), the psychodynamic counsellor does not go simply by appearances. There are legitimate reasons for clients failing to keep time and appointments; but the psychodynamic approach tends to look deeper, to see if there is any *other* reason, which is disguised by the more obvious excuse. It is sometimes possible to interpret poor time-keeping as a character trait. Alternatively, a client may come late (having delayed setting out for the bus) because of her or his reluctance to see the counsellor – perhaps there is something on her or his mind which is painful to talk about, and yet difficult to avoid discussing. Another possible reason is that the client is annoyed with the counsellor. If the counsellor has started late or unavoidably been absent, or if the counsellor has not provided an instant solution, this can lead to disappointment and a 'tit-for-tat' response of letting the counsellor down, or keeping him or her waiting. Missing a session can result from the counsellor 'missing' something important that the client was trying to say, or from making a mistake, perhaps putting across an interpretation in a too judgmental tone of voice. Sessions can also be missed prior to or following the counsellor's own holiday break. Leaving a session early can result from feelings coming too close to the surface, and the client not wanting to show them; or from the need to reject the counsellor before the client feels pushed out at the end of the session by the counsellor. Early termination of a contract can also be a sign of wanting to avoid the closing session, with attendant feelings about ending, or because the client has reached a point where more difficult material, not yet discussed, would otherwise come on to the agenda. 'The flight into health' ('I'm much better now') is particularly evident when the client seeks to break off counselling in the second or third session – the psychodynamic counsellor mistrusts 'miracle cures'.

These are possible explanations for a client's misuse of time, but I would neither wish to suggest that they form a comprehensive list, nor that they can be applied indiscriminately in unthinking interpretations. The psychodynamic counsellor bears these possibilities in mind, waits to see if there is any further evidence that might make an observation of resistance tenable, and tentatively suggests a reason for the client's consideration. Sometimes the counsellor is wrong, but those learning to use the psychodynamic approach are frequently surprised when such possibilities, suggested perhaps during supervision, turn out to have some substance. Given the opportunity to reveal his true feelings the client might well say, 'Yes, actually I did feel rather annoyed with you last week when you couldn't make time to see me on a different day.'

OFF AND ON WITH KARL

Karl, whom I predicted from the initial assessment (pp. 72–4) was going to be a difficult client, provides some examples of the difficulties of making a contract, and of handling issues of time, which in the end gave some hints of a psychodynamic explanation.

We had ten minutes to go in that first session when I offered Karl the choice of another meeting. 'You said earlier that you were giving this a try; do you feel it would be helpful to come next week?' I was hesitant about offering any more than one session at this stage.

'I don't think so.'

'I've not been able to sort you out, as you wanted?'

'No, I'm grateful to you for listening to me. I don't think I want to commit myself to anything more. I can manage. . .'

I felt a little anxious about him going it alone, but at the same time had no clear idea what his own hesitancy was about. I had myself to some extent shared in that hesitancy, and offering only one session illustrated my doubt. I used the remaining minutes to look back with him over some of the story he had been telling me, bringing the single meeting with him to as tidy a close as was possible.

The next week Karl rang and asked to see me urgently, but when I got the message and telephoned him back he said that it was 'a slight panic but I'm feeling fine again now.' 'You want to see me, but you don't want to see me,' I said over the telephone, spelling out his ambivalent feelings towards me and counselling. 'It's your decision, but might we still meet?'

Karl nonchalantly said he would think about it, and that he would let me know. He started to talk about his daughter, but I made my own limits clear. I interrupted him. 'Karl, if you want to meet, you can tell me about your daughter then. But I can't offer you counselling on the telephone. You contact me if you would like to talk more.' After brief good-byes on either side, I rang off.

A month later Karl's name appeared in the appointment book, but he failed to keep his appointment. Normally, in the middle of a contract, a counsellor who charges fees would still request payment for a session missed without prior notice (unless, of course, the client for good reason was unable to let the counsellor know). However, with no contract yet agreed, and in any case the attempt to reach me fraught with ambivalence, I did not wish to ask Karl for the fee. Instead, I wrote to him, wording my letter carefully, re-iterating his uncertainty about coming, and suggesting that if he could come just once we might discuss what made him so anxious about seeing me.

Karl made another appointment, arrived fifteen minutes late, and came in with a paper bag in his hand which he thrust at me. Apologising profusely for causing so much trouble, he asked me to accept 'this small gift'. It was a copy of Kafka's *Metamorphosis*. I put the book on the low table by his side, and asked him what it was that the book said about him which he was unable to tell me himself.

I need only summarise the rest of the session, in which Karl told me first about the book, and only later linked it to himself. Some mornings he awoke and felt a different person; at least not a different person, but the person he had been when he was in prison. It was these experiences which had made his friend suggest he see me, and it was such an occasion which had preceded his call to me after the first session. But the intense feelings of being trapped inside himself passed as rapidly as they came on, and he no longer then felt the need for help.

I suggested that coming to see me when he felt his normal self involved the risk that talking about his experience would push him back into feeling trapped; that he really wanted to be free, and not pinned down by any commitment to see me. Though he had come to see me originally to free himself from those inner feelings of being trapped, he also felt threatened by me, and angry with me because he thought I was trying to get a hold on him. His book was a way of trying to say sorry for messing me around, but I had much rather he took the book back, because he did not need to appease me. I could try to help him with the things that frightened him, but he was free to choose whether he wanted that or not.

Karl suggested meeting occasionally, when he felt bad. I pointed out that in fact I could not guarantee to be available at such times; and that in any case making occasional appointments was probably a way of trying to avoid what might appear a routine, and that routines perhaps made him feel robbed of his hard-won freedom. He wanted to be the one in control, and did not want to give me any control over him. At least I seemed to have struck a chord, because Karl agreed to meet for the next six weeks, and to stop then, because he would then be caught up in the final preparations for his daughter's wedding.

COMMENTS ON KARL

This was a difficult start to the counselling contract, and Karl was not a good time-keeper thereafter. I was sure that coming late meant more than any of the excuses he gave, but it was not clear what his lateness meant, other than a continuing need to feel in partial control of the time with me. With some clients I might have confronted the lateness, and asked them what they thought it meant. With Karl I felt that pushing too hard could be counter-productive. As it turned out, six weeks did not get us very far, but a crisis after his daughter's wedding had a remarkably healing effect.

The missed session, and the book he brought to the second session, briefly illustrate the question of fees, and also the significance of gifts brought by the client. As in all psychodynamic work, nothing that happens or fails to happen is without potential significance, including what may appear to be merely a necessary and practical transaction such as monthly fees. The question of fees, and the psychodynamic significance of paying and withholding money, is an area which I can only allude to; but although such an issue may appear to apply only to private practice (where psychotherapy is more likely to be offered than counselling), it is a factor to be borne in mind in the voluntary sector, where the fee may be a donation, and paid to a receptionist rather than to the unpaid counsellor; or in some counselling services, where the absence of a fee can create a sense of 'debt' in the client, felt keenly as owing to the counsellor for being so helpful, but unable to be discharged through the 'gift' of money (Monger, 1998). Some people believe that counselling is taken more seriously when it involves some financial cost to the client, although there are conflicting opinions about this amongst psychodynamic counsellors.

Karl may have found it difficult to 'give' himself into the hands of the counsellor, but he provides the reader with a continuing example of resistance in the counselling process. It is this important area to which I now turn.

5

THE MIDDLE PHASE OF COUNSELLING: MEETING RESISTANCE

CONFRONTATION

Counselling consists of much more than attentive listening and empathic responses. The 'tea and sympathy' image which some people have of counselling shows ignorance of the way in which all counsellors (at the right time) confront their clients with aspects of themselves that the clients would often prefer not to see or to talk about. Counsellors offer no soft option. The previous chapter has already demonstrated the need to be firm on limits of time, while simultaneously trying to understand the meaning of the necessity of boundaries to the client.

The issue of time and boundaries has already raised the subject of resistance, and the way in which lateness, missing sessions, leaving a session early, or deferring a painful topic until the end of a session, all demonstrate the possibility of the client's reluctance to express certain thoughts and feelings to the counsellor. Such patterns of behaviour sometimes indicate that the client is aware of thoughts and feelings which cannot be expressed openly to the counsellor. The client therefore adopts tactics (which he or she hopes appear reasonable and will not be questioned) to avoid having to mention certain topics in the session.

At the same time, some behavioural patterns, and some ideas and feelings, are unconscious – that is, the client is not aware of them, or is so dimly aware of them that only when attention is drawn to them might they be acknowledged. Other people, however, including the counsellor, are more aware of some of the client's patterns of thinking and behaviour than the client is. If such patterns can be acknowledged by the client, changes in behaviour or attitudes are sometimes possible – although not necessarily easy to effect.

In drawing attention to (or technically 'confronting') these patterns, a counsellor is aware that what he or she has to say to the client may come as a shock, may be experienced as painful, and may be taken as criticism. Confrontation is therefore a skill in itself, requiring attention to its possible effects. Well expressed, and calmly put across, good confrontation may temporarily sting, but at the same time bring relief to the client. The effort of denying (consciously or unconsciously) thoughts and feelings can create considerable inner tension, which can be eased following the acknowledgement of ideas and emotions previously denied access to consciousness or denied expression.

Confrontation is often difficult for the person who is learning the skills of counselling. Counsellors are afraid of hurting their clients by drawing attention to painful feelings, or they worry lest drawing attention to their perceptions of the client's traits will be taken as judgement or criticism. Counsellors may even need to be liked themselves, to be needed by their clients, and so hold back from speaking what they secretly think and feel, for fear that the client will walk out and not come back. Counsellors have their own forms of resistance, emerging from their own fears and feelings, which may be described as their counter-transference to their clients. This is more fully explained in the next chapter.

USING THE COUNSELLOR'S RESPONSES

An effective first step towards learning how to express ideas that are challenging to the client, is for a counsellor to think what he or she would really like to say to a particular client if, as it were, the counsellor did not have to pull punches. This can only be done when the counsellor is open to his or her own real feelings, and has broken free of an idealised self-image of being patient and gentle at all times and with all people. Counsellors are not saints, and they need to get in touch with what a client really evokes in them.

An honest, 'no-holds-barred', but unspoken response to a client provides the counsellor with raw material from which to frame a responsible confrontation. The counsellor's 'gut' feelings can provide the main point which needs to be put to the client. The counsellor may have to disentangle particularly strong feelings in order to assess whether they are genuinely evoked by the client, or whether they represent the counsellor's own difficulties with certain types of people. Once these two steps have been taken, the counsellor can work out how to put across the main thrust of the confrontation in a form of words which the client can hear without feeling too criticised. If the client feels attacked, he or she may simply deny what the counsellor has said, without stopping to consider whether it is true or not.

I can illustrate this process by further reference to Karl's problems with time, referred to in the last chapter. He had agreed, the reader will remember, to meet for six weeks, but the first week he arrived late, and the next two weeks he came later each time. I was anxious initially to help him to see me, and did not want to appear to impose any restrictions on his freedom, because this might remind him of his prison experience. However, I found myself feeling more and more irritated with him for wasting my time, when I knew there were other people who wanted to see me who would probably use the 'hour' more advantageously. The time had come to confront him with his lateness.

What did I really want to say to Karl – no holds barred? As I thought about my feelings, I wanted to say, 'I'm fed up with you mucking me around; there are people who could use this time better than you, who really would appreciate it.' I recognised that my feelings were strong because I like to be punctual myself, and resent people who appear too laid-back about time and commitment. I knew I would need to keep the resentment and irritation out of my voice. I did not think that Karl was simply someone who had a relaxed attitude to time, the sort of person I might in some way envy. I wondered then how to turn my original thoughts into a confrontation which expressed how Karl might be feeling.

A counsellor can afford to wait, and compose an appropriate confrontation, and indeed it is better that he or she should do, rather than prematurely express a cavalier sentiment. If something is worth saying, the client will sooner or later present the counsellor with an opportunity to express it. I wondered whether Karl's lateness was because he was 'fed up' with me (in the same way as I was fed up with him); or whether he was disappointed that I had not proved as 'good' as other people had led him to believe (and to which he had referred early on in our first meeting). I wondered if he had sensed that I did not 'appreciate' him as much as I did clients who more readily used the opportunity for counselling. I thought of expressing my confrontation, therefore, in one of these ways.

I had to wait for an opportunity to make the confrontation. It came when Karl said, coming late for the third time, 'You must be getting fed up with me. I'm a bit of a trial, aren't I?' I integrated my existing thoughts with the particular expression he had used. 'I am wondering whether your lateness means you are getting fed up with me; I have a feeling that you wanted to give me a trial, and that I'm not helping you as much as you hoped?' Karl disagreed; but the next week he was only a few minutes late!

DEFENCES AND RESISTANCES

Confrontation is common to the approach used by all the major counselling orientations. What perhaps distinguishes the psychodynamic approach is the recognition that there are often good reasons for a client's defences, and that the barriers that impede development towards mature relationships and attitudes frequently have to be understood and acknowledged before a person will let them down. Analysis of resistance is a major part of the psychodynamic technique, freeing clients (where it is successful) to understand more of themselves, and releasing them to make the changes which they wish.

Defences are strategies which a person employs, either knowingly or unknowingly, in order to avoid facing aspects of the self which are felt to be threatening. Resistances are the expressions (or tactics) of the defences, particularly used by those employed in the counselling relationship. Both defences and resistances serve a definite and, in some ways, a positive purpose, defending people either against feelings which are too strong and threaten to overwhelm them or others; or against the self-criticism of a punitive and persecutory super-ego (or conscience). The positive aspect of defences is that, when they work, they protect people sufficiently from themselves (or from their fantasies about other people), and enable them to lead a fairly normal life, even if it is a life which is in some respects restricted or impaired.

Karl's resistance to coming to see me was an expression of his defence against feelings emerging, as they did, at odd moments. They felt beyond his control, threatening to overwhelm him and render him liable to admission to a mental hospital. Going into such an institution was for him far too much like the prison experience, which he remembered with such bitterness and fear. So, on the one hand, he wanted me to help him at times of desperation, when the defences broke down, and he felt unable to cope; on the other hand, he feared that seeing me, and talking about what most troubled him, would confront him with the very feelings he wanted to escape.

Sometimes, as the meanings of defences are understood, they in some sense not only conceal but also reveal some aspect of a person's difficulty. Freud suggested that what was repressed could not go on being held back, but that it had to break out somewhere else, like a river dammed upstream has to find a route to an outlet lower down its course. The concepts behind much of Freud's language (that of hydraulics and physical energy) are indicative of the particular scientific climate in which he worked. Yet there is still some validity in that image, and in his idea that anything that is repressed ironically finds a way of showing itself *through the very defences* which are unconsciously employed to keep the repressed at bay. Technically this is known as 'the return of the repressed'. In Karl's defensiveness about coming to see me, he was also providing me with clues about his feelings of being trapped. His resistance threw light on the way his imprisonment had also threatened to overwhelm him, when he had been unable to escape the feelings which had been (and even now occasionally still were) so strong.

Defences and resistances may be identified by technical psychodynamic terms (see below), but what they attempt to mask or hide differs from person to person. Thus Hannah's initial defensiveness about coming to counselling was lest I, like others before me, pay too little attention to her needs, or in some way satisfy my own demands at her expense. Karl was even more resistant to seeing me, but his anxieties were lest I give too much attention to him, and so entrap or enmesh him in overwhelming feelings. Another way of putting it is that it felt threatening to Karl to become dependent. This was less worrying to Hannah, although what she feared was being let down. Her defensiveness (for instance against showing her anger towards her grandfather) indicated that part of her anxiety was also about becoming independent.

Because defences serve a purpose, the psychodynamic approach is one which respects defences in two ways. The first is that some defences appear to work satisfactorily enough not to need attention being drawn to them; this is especially true of supportive counselling, where the main aim is to strengthen the ego and so help a person to cope with her or his situation. Exploration of deeper fears and feelings is deliberately excluded from the counsellor's agenda when working in this supportive mode, and such fears are handled cautiously by the counsellor if the client brings them up. Unfortunately, Karl's initial defensiveness militated against him accepting the supportive relationship which I was offering, and the resistance had to be confronted if I was to succeed in helping him to meet with me. Once he started to come, I preferred to support his central ego in building up a new life, than to risk probing too deeply into his past experiences, since these appeared to immobilise him and prevent his adaptation to a new life of freedom.

The second way in which the counsellor shows respect of defences and resistances is in the way they are confronted. Meeting a defence head-on often leads to the strengthening of the defence, and to further resistance. Where the reason for a defence can be understood and interpreted, it is more likely that clients will begin (albeit slowly) to remove their own defences. Where a defence or resistance cannot be understood, the counsellor gently explores the reasons for it. I illustrate this aspect of handling defences and resistances below.

DEFINING DEFENCES

Both Freud and his daughter Anna described what the latter called 'the mechanisms of defence' (Freud, A., 1968); some of the terms they used, like projection or denial, have entered into popular psychological language or even into everyday speech. The technical terms used in psychoanalytic thought invariably have limitations, in that they are defined slightly differently by different authors. The language about defences is no exception, because some of the defences, as seen in practice, sometimes fit two or more theoretical categories. In his encyclopaedic work which appears to cover every symptom or presenting problem one can think of, Fenichel, otherwise so precise in his detailed explanations of the causes of neurosis, writes on the subject of defences: 'There are no sharp lines of demarcation between the various forms of defence mechanism' (1946: 153). His remark encourages me to attempt to illustrate in Figure 5.1 a possible construction of the defences that I describe in this section, showing the way in which many of them interweave.

The value of using these terms is that they provide a shorthand language for communication between practitioners of counselling and therapy, and (particularly in the context of training) help to extend a counsellor's awareness of the different strategies which people in general, and clients in particular, adopt to avoid acknowledging painful feelings and thoughts.

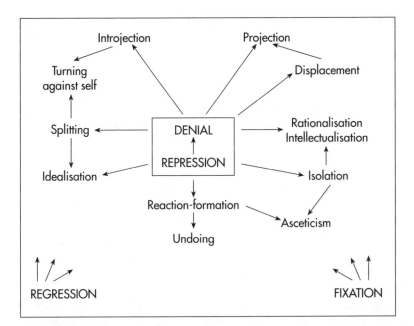

(Regression and fixation may involve any of the above defences as part of their expression, e.g. isolation or asceticism by the fixated person, unable to progress into sexual expression; or idealisation when a person regresses to an infant-like attitude to significant others.)

FIGURE 5.1 *The interweaving of the defences – a possible pattern*

Projection describes the way in which we ascribe to someone else a feeling or characteristic which is also our own, but which we do not appear to be able to acknowledge as ours. Colloquially this might be described as 'the pot calling the kettle black'. Karl, in the example used above, said, 'You must be getting fed up with me. I'm a bit of trial, aren't I?' He may indeed have felt this was true, but at the same time he was projecting on to me feelings of being fed up with me, which he could not express in case he appeared to criticise me, and lose my respect. Projection is a common defence, one which many people recognise others using, even if they are less aware of it in themselves! Projection is sometimes accompanied by condemnation of the other person. This may indicate that one reason why the particular aspect criticised in another cannot be personally owned is because, if it were, it would elicit the same sense of self-condemnation, and therefore perhaps of shame or guilt, as is experienced in the condemnation of other people.

The reverse of projection is *introjection*. While this is a defence which can impede the development of self-esteem and maturity, it is also a positive feature of personal development. Indeed, in this sense it is an essential part of healthy human development: it all depends what the growing child and adult introjects. A baby, for instance, not only takes in the food which the nurturing parent offers, but also 'absorbs' (in the process of being held and fed) some of the qualities of that person. All this is necessary as a foundation for psychological health, as well as for physical health, because early relationships feed a young child in a variety of ways. Positive and negative features of those relationships can be taken in, or introjected, although obviously not only in the first few months of life. As an example of negative introjection at a slightly later time, a punitive conscience suggests identification with and introjection of a fiercely judgmental parent. So, in introjection, a child may adopt the attitudes of an aggressive parent towards the self, and yet at the same time preserve the positive image of the parent by only seeing the parent as kind and loving.

Such an example suggests that this defence is similar to the defence of *turning against self*, although turning against self involves an extra component, in which the child's own aggressive feelings towards the parents are not permitted to reach their target, but boomerang back on the self. The person who is frequently self-condemning may therefore simultaneously introject unconsciously the criticism of a judgmental parent, while fuelling that self-condemnation with aggressive feelings towards parents and authority figures, that have to be denied consciously, and are only permitted expression by being turned back against the self.

The most common reason for any defence is attempting to keep contradictory (or ambivalent) feelings for the same person separate, because it seems impossible at one and the same time to feel, for example, love and hate for the same person. Defences partially resolve the problem of loving the person you also hate, or hating the person you also love, and of coping with negative feelings which threaten to damage a relationship, while at the same time trying preserve the good relationship. This is seen *par excellence* in *splitting*, which is a combination of *projection* and *denial*. Again, Karl provides us with an example. At my first meeting with him he relayed to me others' opinions that 'you're good' and a sentence later described what the astrologer had said as 'rubbish'. This was more than an attempt to flatter me or to stop me getting angry with him (which flattery often seeks to do). Karl found it difficult to conceive that although I was apparently 'good', I might also say things which were not helpful, which then might make *him* angry with *me*. So he praised me and ran the astrologer down. Splitting is a very common reaction towards different helpers, and one counsellor may be played off against another in this way.

I do not suggest that any criticism of another helper is necessarily inappropriate, but the counsellor's desire for her or his own self-esteem can lead him or her to accept such remarks at face value, without considering whether the client is splitting between one therapist who is seen as all good and another who is seen as all bad. Failure to consider such a possibility sometimes leads to clients breaking off counselling, unable to express their negative feelings about the counsellor as they gradually come to the surface. Karl's 'flattery' was a warning to me that although I might be praised at one time, I could easily find myself run down (to another helper) the next!

Such praise of others is sometimes exaggerated, and is seen in the defence of *idealisation*, a defence often employed against acknowledging negative feelings towards a person. Such a person (or sometimes an ideology) is elevated to a point which is close to worship or idolisation. In the counselling setting this applies not just to the counsellor (or sometimes to a previous helper), but is also heard in respect of parents, teachers, or lovers. Nothing they do or did appears wrong, and in the face of such a description the counsellor struggles to locate a reason for the client feeling the way he or she does. If the counsellor swallows what the client says, it appears that any emotional upheavals in the client's upbringing or in present relationships have to be ruled out as an explanation for her or his discontent. Underneath the idealisation, however, there often lurk darker feelings, that the client is as yet unable to acknowledge. Apparent criticism of others is fiercely rejected, even if vehement denial suggests at least the possibility to the counsellor that negative feelings are somewhere present.

Denial, like any of the defences, can be sincerely expressed, with no deliberate attempt intended to deceive either the self or the counsellor. Sometimes a client denies the correctness of a counsellor's interpretation of feelings because it is difficult to tell the counsellor that the suggestion was right; but equally, the client can be unaware of the suggested possibility. Their denial is sincere. To persist with an interpretation when the client denies it is a waste of effort. The counsellor was either completely wrong, in which case some re-thinking is called for, or the counsellor put the point across at the wrong time or in the wrong way, in which case he or she has to wait for another, more relevant, opportunity. Denial is one of the most difficult defences to get through, and evidence to support an interpretation is both desirable and frequently necessary. 'You say, "No I'm not angry", Hannah, but you're gritting your teeth as you say it, and you almost stamped on the floor. You do seem angry, but perhaps you're angry with me for making the suggestion . . .' Denial, like repression, is a constant factor in all the defences, and for this reason I have placed these two terms at the centre of Figure 5.1. Repression or denial take place, initially, against an unwelcome thought or feeling; and then other defences are used to keep the feared idea or emotion at bay.

Displacement is another common defence, and describes the process of expressing feelings towards a different person or object, at an emotional distance, rather than towards the person to whom they should properly be directed. It is commonly seen in the man or woman who returns from work, having been told off by the boss, who slams the front door, flings down the newspaper, and shouts at the children. While there is clearly some introjection here of the angry boss (in other words, identifying with him and copying his behaviour), the anger with the boss is also taken out on, or displaced on to, those at home. Positive feelings can similarly be displaced: for example, stroking the cat when it would really be rather nice to be stroking your partner. On the whole, the positive displacement of feelings is less harmful, and acts as a means of gaining some satisfaction when feelings cannot be satisfied in a more direct way. Indeed, Freud put forward the controversial idea that this kind of positive displacement can be seen in the development of civilisation, where art, science, technology and knowledge of all kinds result from the displacement (or sublimation) of the sexual feelings implicit in creativity and curiosity.

Displacement also provides a constant series of possible clues to unspoken feelings in the counselling relationship. Some of what a client talks about in her or his life outside the counselling session (particularly about feelings and thoughts towards and from other people) is capable of being linked to the counselling itself. Reference to 'being fed up with work' might indicate that the client is getting 'fed up with counselling'; reference to 'people don't understand' can be a reference to 'you, the counsellor, don't understand'; reference to 'I find it difficult to talk to people' can mean that the client also finds it difficult to talk to the counsellor. There is always the possibility that such references are oblique, veiled, and defensive ways of describing conscious and unconscious feelings in the counselling. They therefore form a significant focus for the counsellor's attention, since they may be telling the counsellor about the therapeutic relationship as well as about the external relationships being described. Sometimes such references can also be linked to past events, and may indicate that the relationship is being experienced as a repetition of the past. In those instances there is more than displacement present: transference is also a possibility, repeating with the counsellor past relationships with important figures. The next chapter explains this latter concept more fully.

Defences not only involve unacknowledged negative feelings towards other people, trying to protect them, or the client's relationship with them, from being spoilt by their expression. They also describe a client's relationship to her- or himself, and the damage her or his own feelings and thoughts might do, if fully acknowledged to the self. Denial and repression clearly protect us from facing feelings within ourselves and about ourselves. *Isolation* is another example of a defence against feelings, where emotions are talked about in a matter-of-fact way. Isolation also refers to the way in which a person avoids anything which might in itself, or through its associations, provide 'temptations' to do what is forbidden or feared. There is a type of isolation, for example, in the way Karl avoided coming to see me, in an attempt to isolate himself from what might prove too great a reminder of his past privations.

Intellectualisation (concentrating on intellectual rather than emotional responses), *rationalisation* (arguing one's way out of accepting the truth of a situation), and *asceticism* (abstaining from pleasurable activities like eating, masturbation or sexual relations) are examples of isolating feelings, and are further examples of defences in their own right. All serve the purpose of protecting a person from the anxiety of being overwhelmed by, or punished for, strong loving or hating feelings.

Isolation also refers to another type of splitting, where one feeling is isolated from its true object, and perhaps displaced or split off on to another. The latter acts only as a means of discharging the feeling (such as the isolation of the sexual expression of loving feelings in a marriage, perhaps discharged with a prostitute). Another common form of isolation is when a person disowns his or her responsibility, such as in the phrase, 'It wasn't me, the devil somehow just got into me.' Children do the same when they invent an imaginary friend who becomes the naughty child if anything goes wrong and the parents get cross, leaving the child her- or himself innocent! ('It wasn't me, Daddy, it was Eric!')

Reaction-formation and undoing are closely related defences. *Reaction-formation* refers to the experience or expression (perhaps in an exaggerated form) of feelings which are the opposite of what is really being felt; such as a person being extremely grateful when they are in fact deep down feeling frustrated but have perhaps not recognised this in themselves); or extremely offhand, when in fact there are strong feelings of affection and gentleness towards another. *Undoing* refers to the attempt (often through actions or busy activity) to ward off unacceptable feelings, or to cleanse the guilt which expressing them has given rise to – known as 'reparation' (repairing the damage thought to have been caused). The person who is obsessionally tidy or involved in compulsive rituals is a good example of this, keeping 'bad' feelings at bay. Karl's presentation to me of the book (when he had missed a session) might be partially seen as defensive 'undoing' of his anger towards me (projected on to me, imagining that I would be hostile towards him). The book was, of course, also a way of communicating some of his terrifying experiences to me – the return of the repressed.

The different defences can be categorised as indicating certain developmental stages. Projection, splitting and idealisation, for instance, are reckoned in psychodynamic theory to be 'primitive' defences, employed in the face of the intense anxieties that arise in early infancy. Reaction formation and obsessional defences such as isolation are more indicative of the toddler (or 'anal') stage. Asceticism is linked by Anna Freud to adolescence. It is worth repeating, however, that there is not a great deal to be gained in psychodynamic counselling from an anxious wish to identify all these technical terms correctly. What is more important is to be able to recognise that defences are almost bound to be employed, to spot how defences can be used, and to seek to understand what they might mean. That is the way to help the client find a way through to the true feelings which the defences mask.

There are two further defences which have clear developmental implications. The first is *fixation*, where in some respects a person has been unable to develop emotionally beyond a certain point. Hannah in certain respects seemed fixated at a point in mid-adolescence, unable to break away from her home and her grandfather, and also fearing to make mature relationships with men. This may be because the next developmental stage appears too threatening (the Peter Pan syndrome, the child who does not want to grow up); or, more likely, because the present stage of development has not yet been satisfactorily achieved. So the adolescent who ascetically abstains from food might do so because increased body-size is an indication of approaching adulthood and mature sexuality. It might be this in itself that appears threatening; or perhaps dependent needs have been insufficiently met in childhood. I suggest possibilities: causality is seldom simple. The various reasons behind presenting problems and defences form an infinite number of permutations. What ultimately makes sense to the client is the only real test of whether or not an explanation is valid.

The other developmentally linked defence is *regression*, where psychological development has apparently proceeded satisfactorily until, under the stress of external or internal factors, a person reverts in attitude or behaviour to an earlier developmental stage. Regression to adolescent behaviour, for example, is sometimes seen in middle-aged men and women, faced with the reality of ageing. Although regression is a defence, it is also a healthy part of normal daily life. Dreaming involves a type of regression, where we go back over past events (of the day before, or even earlier) and re-live them in sleep, as a way of settling them and moving forward again. Some activities, such as playing games, have a regressive and usually quite harmless element to them, re-capturing the excitement of the child's world.

Regression can then be a conscious choice, permitted or encouraged in the knowledge that it involves a temporary state of rediscovering pleasurable aspects of childhood. The sort of regression which often brings people to counselling and therapy consists of experiences which they have not chosen, and which tend to make them feel discomfort and vulnerability. They sometimes feel as if they have lost many of their adult ways of coping. Karl, in his episodic feelings of being a different person, was in fact re-living some of his prison experiences, because of the stress which his daughter's wedding was causing him. In order to locate the stage of life to which problems and symptoms point when regression or fixation are employed as defences, the psychodynamic counsellor needs to learn about personality development. Erikson (1965) sets out psycho-social stages very clearly. I have myself moved away from stage theories to look at the way in which different themes run through life, with early and later experiences reflecting similar issues (Jacobs, 1998).

Forms of Resistance in Counselling

Understanding the range of defences which a person experiences under stress, or in the face of unacceptable feelings, is only part of the psychodynamic counsellor's task. It is equally necessary to become aware of the ways resistance can be shown in the counselling relationship; and to ask oneself, as with defences, what a particular form of resistance might mean, to ascertain what feelings and thoughts are being kept at bay. In this way it may be possible to explore with the clients what it is that makes particular feelings and ideas so difficult to acknowledge. When they can be owned, they can often be integrated as a valid and indeed healthy part of the self.

Many of the defences described above can be translated directly into forms of resistance shown to counselling or to the counsellor. Projection is often seen in phrases used by the client such as: 'You must think I'm dreadful', where the client imagines what the counsellor thinks about her or him, even though the counsellor has said nothing critical. Idealisation can be directed towards the counsellor, and may sometimes indicate that the client (unconsciously perhaps) feels antagonistic towards the counsellor, or puts all his or her own potentiality into the counsellor. Denial is often heard in the 'No . . . but' or 'Yes . . . but' responses from clients to attempts on the part of the counsellor to make helpful interventions. Intellectualisation is common in more educated clients, although rationalisation can occur in anyone.

Another form of resistance in counselling is passivity and silence in a client who normally talks freely in counselling. (The extremely passive client, as explained in Chapter 3, is unlikely to make effective use of counselling.) Sometimes a client talks about many trivial issues, or reports the week in such detail that the counsellor feels that more spontaneous feelings are being kept at bay. The need to control what they say is also seen in clients who come each week with 'a little list' of things to talk about. Acting out (see p. 71) is sometimes a form of resistance, particularly against expressing feelings about the counsellor. The way in which time is used (as was described in Chapter 4) can also be an indication of resistance: coming late, missing sessions, or terminating counselling earlier than arranged.

One reason some clients give for finishing counselling is because they feel so much better. Psychodynamic counsellors ask themselves (and, less directly, their clients) how genuine such a change is, because 'flight into health' is a particular form of resistance. Although certain feelings have pushed their way to the surface in the form of symptoms or problems, another part of the personality resists letting the feelings come any further, and so appears to overcome the symptoms. Such a dynamic illustrates how complex the personality is, with different parts of the same person working for and against each other.

On the other side of the coin is a form of resistance known as 'gain from illness'. In counselling, this is likely to show itself when the client's initial problem, having been fairly well resolved during the course of counselling, suddenly flares up again when the end of counselling is arranged or is at hand. Alternatively, new problems occur, just as the counsellor thought that the client was ready to finish. Such difficulties seem to say to the counsellor, 'You can't let me go when I'm feeling like this', and can be a way of resisting both the ending itself, and also the negative feelings attached to ending (see Chapter 7).

It is useful to draw a distinction, as Kennedy and Charles do (1989: 112–19), between the resistant and the reluctant client. They use the term 'reluctant' to describe people who do not want counselling, and attend, for example, only because someone else has asked them to. With such clients it is very difficult to enlist their support in trying to understand and work through resistances and defences to counselling, because their minds are more on the whole dynamic of being sent, and having to obey orders, or bow to pressure. Kennedy and Charles suggest that in such instances it may be necessary for the counsellor to make sufficiently empathic a response to the client's reluctance, to make counselling a possibility at a later date, when the client might choose it. Resistance, unlike reluctance, is what clients show despite their wish to make changes and despite their belief that counselling is the best way to effect these.

INTERPRETING DEFENCES AND RESISTANCES

Whatever name the counsellor gives to the indications that clients may be defending themselves against feelings, or resisting the counselling process, it is crucial that defences and resistances are confronted sensitively, and with as much explanation as is possible about their meaning. When the time is right to draw attention to a defence or to resistance, a good psychodynamic approach is to point out to the client the form of defence/resistance (perhaps with a definite example of it), and then to offer either a good reason for it (if the counsellor has such an idea), or an invitation to explore the reason for it. The reason for a defence nearly always includes a client's fear or anxiety about the effect of expressing particular thoughts and feelings.

Karl, for example, made a time to see me, failed to appear, and then turned up late. As the session went on I began to see how the feelings of being trapped (by making a contract for a series of sessions) echoed his feelings about being trapped in prison, and being trapped inside terrifying experiences. Karl demonstrated his resistance by not keeping his appointment, and then by coming late; the reason was not because he was being deliberately awkward, but because he was frightened of being trapped. So

I put it to Karl, during that second session, 'I am trying to understand what is worrying you so much. I think you're frightened that I am going to pin you down in some way, and I think that may be why you missed last time, and came late today. Do you think that's a possibility?'

Had I not understood (or thought I understood) what the resistance was about, I could have invited Karl to speculate upon it with me. In that case I might have said, 'Karl, there's something I don't understand. There's clearly a problem of coming to see me, missing the last session, and coming late today. I wonder what you are frightened of here?' Seeking a reason with the client is less easy to do when the defence or resistance is unconscious, and the feelings they fear are buried deep inside them. In such instances it is often only the accurate interpretation which frees the defence, and permits the feared feelings to emerge.

Confrontation, therefore, may involve:

1. looking for the resistance or the defence which the client is employing;
2. drawing attention to it;
3. (a) suggesting an explanation for it, which
    i. recognises the client's anxiety,
    ii. if possible identifies the feeling or thought which is being resisted, and
    iii. invites the client to confirm or reject the interpretation;
   (b) alternatively the client's anxiety is recognised, and the client is invited to suggest what feelings or thoughts are being resisted.

A LONGER EXAMPLE: HANNAH

During the third session, Hannah told me more about their eviction from their London home, and how they had come to the town in which she now worked, in a temporary job, where she earned just enough to keep grandfather and herself in a small flat. She was still depressed, but I began to feel that much of what she was now describing was factual information, without much feeling.

The fourth session began with a few minutes' silence, and an apparent reluctance to start. I broke the silence by asking what the difficulty was about saying anything. Hannah replied after a further minute or two: 'There's something I haven't yet told you.' 'What makes it difficult to tell me?', I asked, concentrating on the resistance first, rather than seeking to draw out what she could not say. 'I don't know,' said Hannah. 'You can't trust me with it?', I suggested, looking rather uncertainly for an explanation since she had been unable to furnish one herself. 'Maybe.' Hannah's voice was very flat, and controlled. 'Perhaps you're afraid that what you want to tell me is going to upset you too much?' Her eyes watered. Faltering, she began:

'That dream I told you about, that the landlord had followed us here. That wasn't true.' Hannah told me how she had discovered that her grandfather was still gambling, going to betting shops while she was at work, wasting the little money they had. It was not the landlord, but grandfather's problem with gambling that appeared to have followed them – as one might expect, because running away from problems is seldom a lasting solution to internal difficulties.

'But you talked about a dream . . . What was that dream about?' I did not think the dream was pure invention.

'I was asleep one night, and actually I was dreaming – nightmarish dreams about falling off towers, and so on. Whether it was the dream that woke me up, or a noise in the room, I don't know, but I was aware of someone opening my bedroom door. It was dark, just a little light coming in through a gap in the curtains, and I could only make out a shadow. I was terrified, I thought it was the landlord and that he had followed us. The shadow moved around the room, and felt over the bedspread. My clothes were on the end of the bed where I had left them, and he was feeling through all my things. Then he felt around more, and I thought he was going to feel for me, but he must have found my handbag, because I heard the clip go, and the rustle of notes being taken out. I couldn't move, I was so frightened.

'I lay still, until the person, whoever it was, slid just as quietly out of the door; and I quietly got up, because I was afraid for grandfather. My heart was banging, but I had to go and see him, so I waited by the door until everything was quiet, and crept along the corridor to his room. I pushed the door open quietly, and then . . .'

Hannah burst into tears. It was a few minutes before she could resume her story, and she told me then how the terror had given way to almost uncontrollable grief (except she had not been able to cry out loud), because she saw that her grandfather was asleep on top of his bed, clutching the pound notes from her handbag in his hand.

Words could scarcely describe the feelings of oppressive grief that had descended on Hannah at that time, and had stayed with her since. She saw her grandfather as someone to be afraid of, to recoil from, and she found it painfully difficult to connect her affection for him with this sinister old man. The rest of that session was an occasion to let those feelings emerge.

The fifth session Hannah returned to the dream, because she *had* dreamed about the landlord wanting to have sex with her, only it had occurred *after* this incident. Generally it is difficult in once-weekly psychodynamic counselling to make as much use of dreams as would be the case in that type of psychotherapy where sessions are more frequent. The richness of dream imagery can give rise to so many different associations in the client's mind that there is little time in one session a week to work on the details of a dream as well as on other current or past events. I felt, however, that in this case the dream was connected intimately to the terrifying experience of the figure in the room, and that grandfather's invasion of her room, her clothes, and her handbag, had been experienced as a type of 'rape'. The dream imagery at one and the same time gave expression to this feeling, but also disguised it. It therefore defended her against the incestuous implications of such thoughts.

This was slow and sensitive work. I can perhaps best summarise our session together, by reporting the main interpretation that I made, which gathered together Hannah's words and my thoughts:

'I think I understand now why you were so concerned about me being a psychoanalyst, and what that meant to you in terms of sex. I think you might be tempted to take what I'm going to say now as confirmation of your fear, as if I were getting too personal about things which are rightly very private to you. But from what you told me last week about that terrifying experience in your room, and what you've told me this week about your dream of the landlord wanting sex with you, I can see a connection, which you're frightened to make for yourself. Your grandfather wanted money, and that was bad enough, but going through your private things feels as sordid to you as if you had had sex with the landlord. You and your grandfather have always been so close, but it feels dreadful that he should force himself so close to you as he did that night. I think the reason you've found it impossible to tell anyone before now is because it was too close for comfort. You're afraid to admit it to yourself, but it was like being raped.'

Working through the defences and resistances which a client employs is difficult to illustrate in one brief example. In these extracts from the sessions with Hannah, the reader should note first of all the careful way in which I tried to handle her hesitation at the start of the fourth session. I looked for reasons for her difficulty in telling me 'something'. In the next session her dream of the landlord wanting sex with her gave me a clue to the way she had experienced her grandfather's intrusion; the dream both concealed and yet also revealed (in the way defences so often do) what it was that was troubling her. The reader will also notice that I referred back in my own mind (and indeed out loud to Hannah) to the enquiry which she had initially put to me, which now provided clues (disguised in her resistance) as to what was troubling her.

Had Hannah been talking about me (the defence of displacement), therefore, when she introduced the incident with her grandfather? In some respects she was clearly not, because these were events which had led to her being so depressed, and seeking help, and occurred before Hannah ever knew me. But her defensiveness about psychoanalysis and sex, and her resistance to me when she first came for counselling, were linked in with her terrible experience, although I could not know that at the time. Furthermore, I felt that talking about these particularly private things, and exposing her feelings to me, together with my 'probing' gently around, implied some parallels between counselling and life outside. Hence, when I said that it was 'as if I were getting too personal about things which are rightly very private to you', I was making an important link between my interpretation and her previous negative sexual experience. I was attempting to forestall any rejection of what I said, as yet another example of 'men!' At the same time I was trying to show her that what was going on between us was more of a co-operative partnership, which might indicate that more positive relationships could exist between two people.

The importance of this relationship between counsellor and client is, like the significance of defences and resistance, another major aspect of the psychodynamic approach. Some of the resistances present towards the best efforts of the counsellor can be better understood by reference to the way in which the counsellor–client relationship is hindered, and yet paradoxically helped, by its transference implications. The centrality of the counsellor–client relationship, which I have by and large taken for granted until this point, merits closer attention.

6

THE MIDDLE PHASE OF COUNSELLING: THE RELATIONSHIP BETWEEN COUNSELLOR AND CLIENT

THE CENTRALITY OF THE THERAPEUTIC RELATIONSHIP

It is gradually being recognised, although it has probably been staring therapists and counsellors in the face since psychotherapy and counselling were first developed as helping disciplines, that what I shall call at this stage the 'ordinary' relationship between the client and the counsellor is probably the most important factor in promoting change, more important perhaps than any real differences in theoretical perspective. Research (reviewed by Durlak, 1979) seems to indicate that, if anything, more effectiveness is perceived by clients in non-professional helpers than in professionals. Others have suggested that experienced practitioners, whatever their theoretical position, have more in common in their way of working as therapists, than experienced and inexperienced practitioners within any one theoretical school.

Lomas (e.g. 1973, 1981) has been particularly critical of the traditional psychoanalytic view of the relationship as somewhat distant, 'blank screen', interpretative, and has promoted the value of the therapist's acting as a real person. 'Ordinary' is a word he frequently uses to describe the therapeutic relationship. And when we examine more closely accounts of the way in which major psychoanalysts have worked, we do indeed find a far greater 'ordinariness' about them (a willingness to relate person-to-person, alongside all their skills of being with and understanding their patients) than we might imagine simply from reading their learned books (e.g. Goetz (1975) on Freud; Couch (1995) on Anna Freud; Guntrip (1975) on Fairbairn and Winnicott; Little (1985) on Winnicott; Hill (1993) on different experiences with Kleinian analysts).

I can imagine that person-centred and some other humanistic counsellors and therapists might wonder what is so extra-ordinary about all this. Is this not what they have said all along, that it is the core conditions, conveyed through the person of the therapist or counsellor, that are all that is necessary for the client's growth and change? Provide the right conditions, and people can flourish. I myself do not dispute much of this, although I do not think that such views take us far enough in understanding the complexity of relationships, that is all relationships, including that between counsellor and client. It is for that reason I prefer the fuller picture which psychodynamic theory has given us, with which to understand the different dimensions of the therapeutic relationship. But at the same time, it is my own understanding, from my practice as a counsellor and therapist, as well as from reflecting upon the growing body of literature from a psychodynamic or psychoanalytic perspective, that we can no longer be content as psychodynamic counsellors to think mainly in terms of transference and counter-transference, as was true of much psychoanalytic thinking from Freud's first cases through to the 1960s. (Greenson's first volume of a never-completed two-volume work on technique and practice is the first indication of the significance of the real relationship (1967: 216–24), and he writes too on the working alliance as well as the transference.)

In my more recent thinking I have come to appreciate Clarkson's five-relationship model (1991, 1994, 1995; her own background is originally traditional psychoanalytic, but she is now more integrative than identified with any single school). In an earlier book (Jacobs, 1993b) I too adopt five styles of relationship, but differ from her on the precise identity of these different ways of relating in counselling and therapy. Here I am tempted to give up counting (!), and instead I look at the different ways in which the relationship between counsellor and client is significant from a psychodynamic perspective. If, as in looking at defences and resistance, it is sometimes a matter of which descriptive terms mean what, my objective here is not to seek cast-iron definitions, but to open up the possibilities for understanding and working with the complexities of the dynamics present in counselling.

THE WORKING RELATIONSHIP

We can perhaps take it for granted that most counsellors, at least as a conscious motive for their work, are concerned with the quality of relationships – theirs with the client, the client's with others, and their own with other people outside the counselling room. We also need to remember that counselling is a professional occupation, whether or not counsellors are paid for their work. For salaried, self-employed or volunteer counsellors alike, there is a job of work to be done, and goals to be set (see Chapter 3). Contracts, time-keeping, notes, and the requirement of supervision, fees or donations all set this relationship on a different footing from a friendship or other such personal relationships.

Clients rightly expect both a level of expertise, and (as Lomas suggests, 1973: 137) 'a person who is practised in dealing with human anguish'. The working relationship that exists between counsellor and client (sometimes known as the working alliance) is essentially one of an adult meeting with another adult, not simply as two equal human beings, who share the problems of living, but also as two people who meet to work together on a problem or set of problems. Individual counselling involves an implicit agreement between two adults (counsellor and client) to co-operate in trying to understand certain less adult and less mature aspects in one of them. This does not mean (although some clients think it does) that the counsellor is fully adult and mature, but that the counsellor recognises his or her limitations and works towards his or her own personal growth elsewhere.

I have described earlier (Chapter 3) the features in the client and in the client's presenting problems which the counsellor attempts to assess in order to decide whether psychodynamic counselling, or a different approach, is most suitable. Essentially these features predict too whether or not a good working relationship is possible, since in the working alliance a client is encouraged to move back and forth continuously between subjective free association and more objective understanding; between 'child'-revealing transference reactions to the counsellor and more adult co-operative work; and between periods of letting the unconscious emerge and more conscious thinking about relationship patterns.

Nevertheless, the working relationship, like the attempt by the counsellor to provide an equal relationship, can be influenced by transference reactions on the part of the client, or counter-transference reactions on the part of the counsellor. Although some clients may initially show readiness and ability to think about themselves, as counselling proceeds some of them react defensively or angrily to interventions, because they are felt as judgmental criticisms (as Karl does in the domestic scene I describe below). Some clients believe that the counsellor really has all the answers and that the counsellor is deliberately withholding, waiting for clients to find them for themselves. The transference implication here is that the counsellor can mind-read and is omniscient, like parents were once felt to be. Other clients cannot express their own opinions, because they feel that to do so would be to intrude upon the counsellor's prerogative. Here the transference seems to be to a feared authority figure, who cannot be questioned or up-staged. Some clients may provoke frustration and unconscious hostility in the counsellor, so that the counsellor begins sessions a little late, or finishes them too early. Here the counter-transference of the counsellor interferes with a good working relationship. Sometimes the counsellor attempts to manage the client's life, so that the over-protective parent–helpless child transference/counter-transference in the relationship places the client in a dependent role in the work, rather than in a collaborative partnership with the counsellor. Such interference is not confined to the working relationship of counsellor and client – it also occurs in the training and supervisory relationship, where the trainee may treat the supervisor in similar ways. Ideally, the learning situation requires a good working alliance between student and trainer or supervisor (Hartung, 1979).

THE EQUAL RELATIONSHIP

Any helping relationship involves two or more people, who, whatever else divides them professionally, share a common humanity. It is in this existential sense that they are equals, sharing in common the joys and sorrows of human life, even if their individual circumstances may mean different joys and sorrows. It is through counsellors understanding themselves as ordinary human beings, partly through their own personal counselling or therapy (felt to be an important part of the experience of the trainee in the psychodynamic approach), that they find relevant personal knowledge that can sometimes be applied to clients' descriptions of their own situations. It is not a question of 'There, but for the grace of God, go I', as the counsellor listens to the client, but 'There am I too'. Even though I do not wish to dwell on this point, I underline it, because in psychodynamic counselling, as much as in any other form of counselling, it is essential that the counsellor is genuine, accepting and empathic.

One of the foremost British writers on the psychodynamic approach, the psychotherapist Guntrip, wrote that the therapist must be a 'whole, real human being . . . and not just a professional interpreter. Only then can the patient find himself and become a person in his own right' (1971: 66). Lomas states unequivocally that 'the crucial need of the patient is to be understood, valued, loved, respected by the therapist as an equal, fellow human being. This is irreducible, it is not simply transference' (1973: 133).

It is not always straightforward in practice, particularly in learning to use a psychodynamic approach, to get the balance right between three aspects: first, holding back in order to allow the client the space to develop his or her own story and associations, and to see where a counsellor's feelings may throw light on transferential and projective aspects of the relationship; secondly, encouraging the client to reflect on what he or she is saying and feeling as an equal participant in the working relationship; and thirdly, essentially being oneself, not allowing the counsellor *persona* to mask ordinary human responses and reactions. Initially, in their training, counsellors often have to be helped to hold back on sharing their different feelings (some helpful, and others unhelpful), because if they continue to do this, they may prevent the client from expressing her or himself more fully. This may seem false and frustrating to the trainee, who feels he or she is being cold and inhuman. As counsellors learn to hold back the expression of their personal reactions and feelings, and find that this increases the client's participation, it is possible for some counsellors to go to the other extreme, and show nothing of themselves. They almost become sadistic in their refusal to allow themselves to appear human. The majority learn, as Kennedy and Charles suggest, that 'maturing counsellors appreciate the fact that what they do in counselling does not ask them to change themselves as much as it invites them to come closer to their best and frequently unrealized selves' (1989: 62). Although a little unrealistic, because most trainees *do* have to learn to hold back on unhelpful responses, the authors are right to observe that with increasing confidence, psychodynamic counsellors can hold the tension between self-disclosure and 'abstinence' (pp. 45–7).

In this aspect of the relationship, as much as in the working relationship, what the counsellor wishes to offer and what a client expects may not always match. Counsellors of different theoretical approaches normally hope to offer an understanding, valuing, caring and respecting milieu for a client. They promote a more equal relationship, whereas some clients want their problems solved, and are impatient with attempts to look at inter-personal factors. Some clients thirst so much for deep human contact that the counsellor's offer of some aspect of her- or himself is seized upon, and raises expectations of a much deeper and intimate relationship than the counsellor or therapist can ever offer. Self-disclosure, as I referred to in Chapter 2 (pp. 32–3), can lead to idealisation. Lomas also records: 'Some of the most painful experiences I have suffered are occasions when I have given my heart to a patient only to find that the sincerity of my behaviour had been understood by him as a triumph of his manipulative power' (1981: 144). The fallibility and ignorance of the counsellor can be turned into rage at the counsellor's apparent unwillingness to help. Most of us in fact cannot see a counsellor, a therapist, or any authority figure as essentially just another human being. We feel a sense of triumph when (despite all our head knowledge that they are no different) those we have elevated to god-like status prove to have feet of clay. Psychodynamic counselling must always promote the equality of the counsellor and client, as an essential basis for counselling to take place; but it is highly unusual for the relationship to function only at that level.

It nevertheless remains one of the aims of counselling to enable the relationship between counsellor and client to become more equal, so that transference reactions and perceptions are largely dissolved. This may well be a somewhat idealistic goal, because the shorter contracts available to clients in many counselling settings mean in practice that such an aim can only be partially realised. There is actually some doubt in psychodynamic theory, which I share, as to whether transferences can ever be totally resolved. Although Guntrip (1971) believes that in therapy the client moves from unrealistic transference relationships to the discovery of what kind of real relationship exists between her- or himself and the therapist, and so to an accurate perception of the therapist in her or his own right, others such as Sandler (1976) believe that complete dissolution of the transference is a myth.

TRANSFERENCE IN EVERYDAY LIFE

In addition to the recognition of the defences and resistance, the psychodynamic approach to counselling has always attached particular importance to what is called 'transference'. This term is used to describe a phenomenon in the therapeutic relationship that was originally felt to be a barrier and defence to the working relationship, where a client treats the therapist or counsellor as if he or she were a parent or lover rather than a helper. Freud's particular contribution to the understanding of transference, after his initial concern about its interference in the process, was to see that it was not a defence as such, but that like defences, it demonstrated 'the return of the repressed'. It could become a way of seeing past relationships come to life in the context of the therapeutic relationship. Hence the therapeutic situation could become a kind of 'living laboratory'. In many instances the feelings and ideas about the counsellor revealed by the transference relationship prove a valuable aid to understanding past relationships, and to re-working what might have gone wrong in the past (although this latter aspect may be better understood as the reparative relationship – see below).

The phenomenon of transference is by no means confined to psychodynamic psychotherapy: if it has any value at all as a concept, we must recognise that it is present in any counselling relationship; indeed, as I suggest below, in any relationship. In short-term counselling there may be less opportunity for the transference to show itself, or for a counsellor to become aware of the particular pattern the client–counsellor relationship; there may also be less opportunity to understand in what particular ways the present relationship is influenced by patterns of reactions laid down in the client's past. But it is still there.

If the term 'transference' was coined by Freud as part of the technical vocabulary of therapy, as a phenomenon it is as old as human existence. It is present in all human relationships, although in everyday situations we tend to respond to the interference of transference reactions by taking what is said and what happens between two or more people at face value, and not seeing the way previous relationships fuel present difficulties. Lomas suggests, however, that the phenomenon is well understood in many close relationships, even if not given a name; and that while it may have once been necessary to adopt the clinical purity of the laboratory in therapy, in order to identify the phenomenon and to study it, transference is now so much part of our understanding of relationships that we do not need to have to use an extraordinary procedure in order to maximise it or utilise it (Lomas, 1973: 138).

There was a good example of the transference phenomenon in everyday life in one session with Karl, when he told me of an incident at home, which was in some ways rather minor, but illustrated, as his initial encounters with me had done, that he was very defensive when anyone appeared to be telling him what to do. His daughter Lucy had commented on his choice of tie, saying that she did not feel it matched his shirt. Karl had flown into a temper: 'How dare you tell me what I should or should not be wearing!' She had responded to his vehement reaction by telling him she was not going to be talked to like that. And so it went on. A row developed, and what had started as a simple observation on her part gave rise to this argument between them. For her part, Lucy probably saw her father's response purely as criticism of her, evidence either of the strain in their current relationship, or of his taking out on her the strains of his present situation (what we might call displacement, referred to in Chapter 5).

This situation could be understood differently, and interpreted in a new light, had Karl added to his original response the phrase: 'You're just like your mother – how dare . . .' etc. Or Lucy might well have said: 'And you're always treating me as if I should be seen and not heard . . . Why do you always put women down?' It is possible to understand Karl's behaviour in this domestic situation as the repetition of a pattern of response that had originated in the relationship between Karl and his wife; and probably before that between Karl as a child and his mother, who (he felt) was always complaining about him. Many such patterns of relating and responding are built up in each of us during the long, impressionable childhood, which is both the blessing and the curse of the human species.

In Karl's situation the argument might not have developed had Lucy been able to stay cool and unpack the tension that was building up between them. She might have said: 'I wasn't criticising you. I'm not like my mother. All right, I know *she* did, but *I* was only pointing out that I don't think your tie goes with your shirt.' But she had her own agenda, and naturally did not like being spoken to in that way. When she was living with relatives after her father's imprisonment and mother's separation, the women and girls were not allowed to contradict the men of the house. Her frustration at that time was re-awakened now by her father's rejection of her comment on the tie; and she burst into tears: 'You never let me comment on anything!' It can be seen how day-to-day relationships can easily be influenced by previous experiences, so that any one of us can, at a particular moment, confuse past and present.

Transference does not only involve negative feelings. Falling in love is a good example of positive transference, where initially those in love see each other as the perfect person, and absolutely inseparable – strong feelings that reflect the early bliss of the mother–baby relationship. The transference involved in such feelings is shown in the fact that these feelings rarely last in such an intense way, but are eventually replaced with more realistic perceptions. Yet transference never totally disappears in any relationship, and when negative transference occurs, as it often does at moments of strain and stress, it can cause real problems.

Although I use the adjectives 'positive' and 'negative' to describe different types of transference in everyday life, based on a simple notion that the feelings may be positive or negative, in psychodynamic counselling and therapy, 'positive transference' is often used to describe a therapeutic relationship where the transference is not too intense, and where it furthers the working alliance: such as the 'faith' which the client puts in the counsellor, or the good feelings a client has about the counsellor, which make the client more open to the work involved. Negative transference tends to be used of the relationship when it is adversely influenced by very strong feelings, whether they are (in ordinary language) 'positive', like admiration of the counsellor, or 'negative' as in deep suspicion of the helper. A 'positive transference' also comes from a client's earlier experience – where good nurturing relationships have promoted the capacity for trusting and co-operative relationships later in life. But even if the transference is 'negative', that is, it gets in the way of the work, it nevertheless provides a way of seeing into the client's past relationships, and to those problem areas that have left the client unable to adapt to the more favourable circumstances of the present. He or she still lives with past suspicions, hostility, envy, over-dependent or over-sexualised expectations of others, etc.

Gosling does not find this classification of positive and negative feelings very helpful, and instead writes about transference in psychotherapy: 'In fact the episodes are always of very mixed feelings; thus, for example, although rivalry has an obvious component to it of opposition and challenge and hostile determination, it also contains an essential component of respect if not admiration' (1968: 9).

REALITY AND TRANSFERENCE

As this chapter develops, and the different ways of understanding relationships become apparent, it is clear that what goes on between a counsellor and client is not to be understood as simple and straightforward. There are conscious and unconscious elements; there is a combination of realistic perception of others, together with exaggerated and distorted images of them, based on the legacy of earlier relationships rather than the reality of the present one. In a post-modern world we are never really sure of anything, especially when relationships are built so much upon mutual perceptions and misperceptions.

In the domestic situation that Karl described there are three different forms of relationship between him and his daughter Lucy. The 'row' reveals two different expressions of what might be called adult-to-adult communication, and two similar examples of child-to-adult communication. Karl's daughter's initial comment – 'I don't really feel that tie matches your shirt very well' – is an expression of adult opinion. Her remark communicates, on an ordinary reality level, what she actually thinks of his dress sense. Had Karl responded to her in a calm way, we could say that these two people were behaving towards each other in a realistic and co-operative manner. We could call this aspect of their interaction a demonstration of 'the equal relationship'.

Another example of an adult way of relating is seen in the expression: 'I wasn't criticising you. I'm not like my mother. All right, I know *she* did, but *I* was only pointing out . . .' Had she said that, Lucy would have been trying to help Karl understand why he was reacting so strongly. She would, in a way, be attempting to help them work together on a problem of communication and understanding between them. We could call this way of interacting 'the working relationship'. It is different from the equal relationship, because the daughter is trying to help her father work on a difficulty in their relationship, rather than them simply sharing their thinking and feeling with each other.

However, a transference relationship also appears in this domestic situation. One example of this is: 'How dare you tell me what I should or should not be wearing!' Karl responded to his daughter as he might have done to his wife, or as the child in him might like to have responded to his mother. He was probably reminded of both of these women by his daughter's remark. There is a second example of a transference relationship, in his daughter's response: 'You never let me comment on anything!' Of course, her response is in some ways quite realistic and appropriate, because Karl's outburst prevented a reasonable conversation. But her cry also contains exaggerated language ('never', 'anything') as well as a strong emotional response (her tears). This distinguishes her transference response from an otherwise calmer, more reasonable reply.

In this example of the row over Karl's tie, both in what actually happened and what might have happened, I have suggested that he and his daughter might have been relating in three different ways in a short space of time: first, on an equal level, talking together; secondly, because the equal level does not quite work, on a working level, looking at a problem of communication; and thirdly, more negatively, both were relating to each other on a transference level.

This way of describing the interaction between two people is to some extent arbitrary, and no communication between people is clear cut. Indeed, because transference is present everywhere, it is often difficult to disentangle transferential and other ways of relating in any one situation. In counselling and therapy these distinctions become more important, especially where transference elements interfere with the working alliance and the equal relationship, and where they may provide clues to unravelling the reactions of the client to significant others.

In fact the interference of the transference can be understood itself in three different ways: transference, counter-transference, and non-transference. I have no wish to make this more complicated than it need be, but I believe each of these elements is important for a more complete understanding of what is happening in the counsellor–client relationship. I take each of these elements in turn.

TRANSFERENCE IN THE COUNSELLING RELATIONSHIP

It is clear, from the qualifications already expressed about both the equal and the working relationship, that transference is ubiquitous. It is present to a greater or lesser degree at some time in all relationships. The counselling relationship provides an opportunity to highlight or intensify transference reactions because, unlike any other relationship, the counsellor tends to keep him- or herself, as an ordinary person, in the background. Similarly, although a counsellor has some psychological expertise, he or she holds back from contributing too much too soon in the working relationship. By keeping quiet, and by listening carefully to what the client has to say, a psychodynamic counsellor often begins to identify a number of possible transference connections. Supervision assists this process of identification of the client's transference. Some of these perceptions will be vague, presenting only a slim opportunity of making a helpful intervention. Such ideas normally need more substantiation before they can be expressed to the client. Other connections are more obvious, such as evidence of past incidents or relationships in the client's life that support a particular interpretation of the transference.

The counsellor does not necessarily have to wait until there is hard evidence, or confine remarks to transference interpretations. He or she can approach a possible transference connection more tentatively, by inviting the client to work on some exploration of transference: for example, as I said at an early point to Karl, 'You appear to be very suspicious of me, as though you aren't sure about my attempts to understand you – I wonder if it would be helpful to look in more detail at what has happened to you that makes you feel so wary here?'

The decision to draw attention to the transference must, however, be a considered one. Longer-term psychodynamic therapy and counselling provide more space and opportunity for the transference to develop, to deepen in its intensity, and to be worked through. The so-called resolution of the transference takes place partly through the client coming to understand (intellectually, and also experientially) what transference is. A cartoon (I think it was in the *New Yorker*) illustrates this combination of 'head' and 'heart': a man is walking down the street, his face glum, a briefcase in one hand, a pocket cassette player in the other. The taped voice in his ear is saying, 'Mr Prentice is not your father. Alex Binster is not your brother. The anxiety you feel is not genuine. Dr Froelich will return from vacation on September 15th. Hang on.'

Drawing attention to the transference, the therapist or the counsellor wants to help the client recognise that present feelings actually *have* got some basis in past situations. He or she also hopes to help the client understand that emotions that might seem exaggerated or inappropriate now, were once normal and appropriate, at the age or during the period when they were first experienced. The counsellor tries to help the client to recognise that there is an 'as if' quality to transference: 'You are reacting to me *as if* I were your parent, and *as you would have done if* you were a child.' Such recognition often takes a considerable time. A counsellor usually has to repeat the same transference observation many times, over many different sessions, because even when the client understands inappropriate reactions to the counsellor intellectually, changing deeply embedded attitudes takes longer. It is in the experience of being with the counsellor, and learning from a different type of relationship (the reparative relationship – see below), that changes are also partly effected.

Clients are gradually helped to see and to learn that some of their most inappropriate (and therefore most uncomfortable) feelings have a rational explanation, that at one time those feelings were appropriate, but more often than not were at that earlier time unable to be fully expressed. Such understanding does not remove feelings, and indeed counselling does not seek to take away the capacity to feel. More often than not counselling enhances the ability to accept and express emotion, but to express it in appropriate ways to the appropriate people. Some clients gradually sense more control over the expression of their feelings; others learn not to fear expressing them.

The therapeutic setting allows strong transference feelings to be experienced and expressed. Whether it is love, hate or any other emotion, clients come to realise that voicing intense feelings does not lead to disruption of the counselling relationship and this in itself often leads to such emotions becoming much less threatening. It is frequently the anxiety that intense love or hate will drive others away that leads people to suppress their strongest feelings. As they realise that the counsellor is not shocked, is not hurt, is not put off, and does not misuse the client's feelings, or does not respond in any other inappropriate or damaging way – in other words, does not repeat the reactions which the client has experienced in the past – feelings become more accessible in other relationships as well.

CONSIDERATIONS IN USING TRANSFERENCE OBSERVATIONS

Drawing attention to the transference, and trying to interpret what it might mean, is governed by some important considerations. The first is that it is better, particularly in counselling (where opportunities for transference interpretation are generally less than in long-term psychotherapy), to concentrate upon exploring or interpreting transference reactions that obviously impede the working relationship. The second consideration is to broaden the whole concept of transference, from the narrow, stereotypical notion of transference that the client falls in love with the analyst, and to look for other transference reactions that might impede the working relationship: 'There are also episodes of falling in hate, falling into rivalry, into admiration, into contempt, etc.' (Gosling, 1968: 8). The transference relationship can feature every type of feeling. Where any of these feelings intrude too much upon the working relationship, the counsellor encourages the client to explore both their inappropriateness and their meaning, and particularly how such feelings might reflect other relationships, past and present, in the client's life.

Whether a particular transference impedes or enhances the counselling relationship depends to some extent on how the counsellor reacts to it (and this involves the counsellor's 'counter-transference' – see below). One of the reasons why it can be valuable to engage in personal counselling or therapy in training is to help counsellors learn about their blind spots, and their own transference difficulties. An intense attachment, unrecognised because a counsellor likes to be admired, will in the end probably cause problems to both client and counsellor. So will the client's negative feelings, if the counsellor is afraid to take them up, because it might appear to 'cause trouble' to do so. Or if a counsellor constantly interprets a client's disagreements with the counsellor's interpretations as examples of negative transference, the counsellor needs to look at his or her own need to dominate the client.

Another consideration to be taken into account in deciding whether or not to share an interpretation with the client, or alternatively to invite the client to explore the transference, is that to do so inevitably draws more attention to the counsellor–client relationship. This can itself lead to intensification of the feelings. Drawing attention to the transference, and focusing on the counselling relationship, gives the client permission to own and express to the counsellor those thoughts and feelings which in other professional relationships are not normally talked about, because they are felt to be either irrelevant, inappropriate, or impolite. So, when I observed, as I did to Hannah at the end of the first session (see p. 83): 'It may seem as if I am having to leave you on your own now for a while, because we have to finish in a few minutes . . .', I was drawing attention to a possible transference link between her feelings of being left on her own after dark by her grandfather, and my stopping the session and leaving her alone in the darkness of her depression. By implication I was saying, 'I find it all right to talk about how you feel about me leaving you in the dark, and you may have similar feelings towards me for doing that, as you did towards your grandfather'.

Likewise, if a counsellor draws attention to more positive feelings in the transference relationship (often *en route* to the exploration of more negative feelings), this too may foster a client's feelings. If a counsellor suggests, 'I feel you're telling me how much you missed me while I was on holiday', he or she is allowing, if not encouraging, the acknowledgement of the client's possible dependency needs. Interpreting the transference carries with it the responsibility of carrying through the implications of allowing such feelings to be expressed. A responsible counsellor cannot legitimately drop a client should the going get too rough or intense as a result of his or her own transference interpretations. Drawing attention to possible transference feelings brings the actual counsellor–client relationship on to the agenda; and can lead in some clients to very strong feelings, such as sexual desires for the counsellor, or to a type of demanding dependency that makes it hard for the client to tolerate the time between sessions.

This wish for an intense relationship is typically known as 'the erotic transference', although I find this a very narrow term, which over-emphasises sexuality, as in the early days of psychoanalysis, and accords less attention to infantile needs. There are, of course, clients who feel such intensity without the therapist or counsellor interpreting anything. Supervision in all these instances is obviously vital, to save damaging the client or the therapeutic relationship. A particular feature of this intense transference has been described by Winnicott as indicative of a deep regression to a time of extreme dependency early in the developmental process. Whereas in more usual transference situations there are *some* elements of the past that can be seen at work in the present, in the intense transference the past appears virtually to take over the present; or as Winnicott puts it: 'In this work it is more true to say that the present goes back into the past and *is* the past' (1958: 297–8). The 'as if' quality of the transference already referred to is much more tenuous in the intense transference, with the client far less able to distinguish appropriate feelings for the counsellor from those which flood in from past frustrations.

This type of client is not appropriate for inexperienced counsellors and therapists but they still need careful handling and sensitive referral to a more experienced practitioner. It may just be possible to provide a supportive, reflective style of counselling, in which the counsellor deliberately holds back from open observation of the transference, or from referring too directly to the counsellor–client relationship. Any expression or action that might provoke too strong a dependency upon the counsellor is avoided, and only those issues are concentrated upon where the client indicates positive progress might be possible.

Even with less disturbed or disturbing clients, it is not always necessary to make clear transference observations. I suspect that a good many psychodynamic counsellors and therapists use their observations of the transference to inform their interpretations and other interventions, without making the possible transferential position explicit. For example, a client may show considerable deference to the counsellor, accepting everything that is said as if it were 'gospel', and as if the counsellor has all the answers. The counsellor may feel, particularly if it is an early session, that it could be off-putting to the client to draw too much attention to this attitude. A psychodynamic counsellor would make the assumption that this deference probably shows itself elsewhere, and will be found also in past relationships. Instead of observing this deference taking place in the session, the counsellor can therefore explore the possibilities of it appearing outside – 'I get the feeling you might give way easily to other people's pressure'; or, 'I am wondering whether it was ever difficult for you to disagree with your parents?'

THE TRIANGLE OF INSIGHT

A transference interpretation, in its fullest sense, can be pictured as a three-sided figure. In fact the expression 'the triangle of insight' in psychodynamic theory describes the aim of a transference interpretation. In the triangular figure (Figure 6.1) there are three points of connection, the present situation (counsellor and client), the present situation (client and others) and the past (normally client and parents). An intervention by client or counsellor, as a contribution to understanding what has been or is being experienced, and that links up any of these points, is called an interpretation. Interpretations appeal partly to the mind and intellect, although sometimes an accurate and well-timed interpretation, or its repetition in different sessions, leads to that kind of knowledge which we can only describe metaphorically as a 'change of heart', 'a vision', a new way of seeing, an 'aha' experience, and a transforming moment.

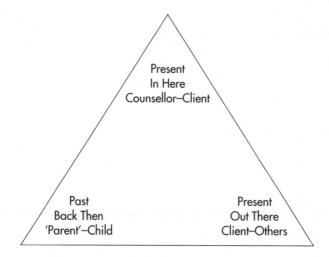

FIGURE 6.1 *The triangle of insight*

Interpretations can be made by client or counsellor – and the counsellor needs to listen carefully for opportunities to support clients in making their own. As early as the first session clients can make connections between past and present, which merit support. They can often be underlined by the counsellor as a possible explanation for why clients feel the way they do. Clients are less likely, at least in early sessions, to make the

connections between their relationship with the *counsellor* and other relationships outside or in the past. Here, bearing in mind the considerations
set out above, the counsellor can take the initiative, so that through well-
timed and relevant interpretations, the client is helped to see all three
connections – back there, out there and in here.

No interpretation, whether it is of the transference, or of resistance and
defence, or of a combination of the two, is a magic spell that miraculously
cures a client. Situations rarely change overnight. Indeed, when on the
rare occasion they do, a psychodynamic reaction tends to be one of suspicion, and makes the counsellor wonder whether the client is using the
defence referred to as the 'flight into health' (Chapter 5): 'I feel much
better this week. I don't need to come anymore. Thank you; you have been
very helpful.'

Change is generally a slow process. Psychodynamic work lays stress on
the constant re-iteration of an interpretation, not as an exercise in 'brain
washing' (although there are some similarities to desensitisation and re-
education in cognitive-behavioural therapy). If an interpretation appears
to make sense to a client, it is probably going to be repeated at intervals,
over a number of sessions, using where possible a variety of phrases and
illustrations to express it, because the 'compulsion to repeat' that Freud
described (1913, 1920: 290–4) arises in relation to later incidents and
events about which the client talks. Each session is likely to throw up further examples of situations that have been presented in past sessions.
However, working through, as this repetition is technically known, does
more than re-iterate words like the tape-recorder in the cartoon referred
to above. 'Working through' also involves, for the counsellor in particular, constant refinement of interpretations so that more subtle and
relevant attention can be given of the client's attitudes and feelings.
Working through consolidates learning, but it also enables a fuller understanding of the client, and by the client, to take place over a period of
time.

TYPES OF TRANSFERENCE

As a way of finding one's way through the feelings which arise in the counselling relationship it is helpful for the counsellor to have a mental picture
of the possible transference implications. Psychodynamic thought, drawing
upon the developmental model of personal growth, provides a classification of styles of transference, which I have developed for practical

application elsewhere (Jacobs, 1998). More detailed use of the transference relationship is a skill which develops later in the practice of counselling, but it is useful to mention here that there are three particular styles of transference, which have their own characteristics: I may over-simplify, but some clients treat the counsellor as a mother figure, some as a father figure, and some as a lover figure.

Such a description is too simple because the maternal or paternal transference can take place whether the counsellor is a woman or a man. The sexual/lover transference demonstrates a different type of transference and may be more gender-related, although same-sex relationships need also to be taken into account in this equation. Although where counsellor and client are of the same gender the transference relationship may include rivalry, it may also involve the wish for an intimate partnership; and while it may be thought that the different genders in client and counsellor could lead to a sexual transference, it may of course throw up all manner of issues to do with male/female relationships. (Issues around homosexuality can be fraught in some psychoanalytic circles, although less so in psychodynamic thinking. They are explored fully in relation to schools of psychoanalytic and psychodynamic thinking in Shelley, 1998.)

The maternal transference might be expressed through thoughts or phrases used by the client in relation to the counsellor, which seem to say, 'hold me, feed me, touch me'; by corresponding anger if the counsellor is seen to fail to meet such demands; or by fear of closeness, or of being 'smothered' by the counsellor.

The paternal transference, a much more common type, is seen when the counsellor is treated as an authority, as someone who knows the answers, who will set down rules, who will give advice and guidance, and who will either be pleased with or critical of the client; or the counsellor will be resisted as an authority figure. 'Yes . . . but' or 'just you try to make me', illustrate the latter type, or 'tell me, advise me, guide me, praise me' the former type of response to the paternal transference.

The lover/sexual partner figure transference is seen in cases where the client wants a special relationship, wishing for, or fantasising about the counsellor as an intimate friend or sexual partner. Alternatively, the client, like Hannah at the first meeting with me, may be afraid that the intimacy of the counselling relationship (where deeply personal and private matters are discussed) will lead to over-intense feelings on the part of the client, or the counsellor, or both.

TRANSFERENCE AND NON-TRANSFERENCE

The over-concentration upon transference in some psychoanalytic technique has obscured the possibility that when a client is referring to others,
outside the therapeutic relationship, he or she may be expressing in an
oblique way concerns about the usefulness of the therapist or counsellor.
Here I draw upon the important corrective to interpreting everything that
is said as 'transference', put forward in recent years by Robert Langs,
and the school of communicative psychotherapy (Langs, 1978; Smith,
1991; Sullivan, 1998). Langs believes that therapists cause damage to their
clients by not listening carefully, and by in one way or other 'breaking the
frame' – the frame being that set of boundaries which is set round the
therapeutic relationship. Here he is not thinking of therapist sexual
exploitation so much as not being a good therapist to the client. He
believes that clients consistently tell stories to their therapists in which
they are trying to inform their therapists where they are going wrong, as
well as where they may be getting it right.

While I think it is possible to over-play this particular card, Langs is
absolutely correct in asserting that our clients seek to tell us what they like
or do not like about the way we treat them. These stories by clients are not
always examples of transference: so that if Hannah were to tell me that
her grandfather is taking no notice of her, she could be saying implicitly,
'*You* are not taking sufficient notice of me'. A traditional psychoanalytic
stance might rationalise such a remark by interpreting Hannah's words as
believing that I was not taking enough notice of her, because that is what
she has come to expect from past relationships, however attentive I may be
to her now. Langs asks us to take what clients say at face value. Perhaps I
have *not* been listening fully to what Hannah is trying to tell me, and she
is telling me this, through her story about her grandfather. Such a possibility was in my mind when, following her story about the dream and the
intruder in her room, I said to her (p. 112), 'I think you might be tempted
to take what I'm going to say now as confirmation of your fear, as if I
were getting too personal about things which are rightly very private to
you'. Langs, I imagine, might tell me that my words 'as if' were misplaced.
He might say I *was* trying to get too personal, and Hannah was warning
me that this was dangerous territory for us both.

I have come to accept that Langs has a valid position, although I do not
go so far as some communicative psychotherapists do in reading nearly all
client communications as this type of non-transference remark (see, for
example, Livingston Smith's responses to a case of mine in Jacobs, 1996a).

COUNTER-TRANSFERENCE

The counselling relationship includes another dimension which bears a close resemblance to transference. Indeed, it is the counter-part to transference: that is, the feelings evoked in the counsellor by the client. As was the case initially with the phenomenon of transference, counter-transference was at first (and for a long time) viewed as a barrier to effective psychodynamic work. It was understood simply as the therapist's irrational and inappropriate reaction to particular clients, or to particular features generally in clients, and therefore a block to insight and understanding on the therapist's part. Counter-transference could only impede his or her ability to practise effectively. Personal analysis was introduced partly to try to overcome this ever-present difficulty. Only later was it realised, as it was with transference, that there are aspects of counter-transference which can be extremely valuable in furthering the course of therapy and counselling, making for even more effective understanding of the client and of the therapeutic relationship.

Counter-transference has come to be used in current thinking as a constant way of monitoring what is going on between the counsellor and the client – sometimes to the exclusion of its original meaning of a transferential and unproductive block in the counsellor. A counsellor's feelings when with, and/or towards, a particular client may result from the counsellor's reactions that belong more appropriately to another part of the counsellor's life, either earlier, or external to the counselling situation. Yet some of a counsellor's feelings may be triggered off by the actual relationship with the client. The double meaning of the same term can lead to confusion, and different expressions have been used to try to describe the complexity of counter-transference reactions. I do not wish to complicate matters further by referring to them here, although the reader can pursue these ideas in Winnicott (1960), Racker (1968), Fordham, M. (1974), Searles (1979) or Maroda (1991).

Counter-transference feelings that impede the counselling relationship might include the counsellor's hostile feelings towards a client, even though the client has done nothing to make the counsellor feel angry; or over-anxiousness about a client, for example, because the client reminds the counsellor of another case where things went badly wrong. The counsellor may not notice some things that a client is hinting at, because of his or her own blind spots. Alternatively, the counsellor can experience inappropriate positive feelings for the client: for instance, becoming over-concerned, unduly kind, or even lax in maintaining counselling boundaries, favouring the client by giving more time than usual, or responding more personally than would normally be felt to be appropriate. The counsellor may even feel unduly attracted to the client, and use the intimacy of the counselling session to take advantage of the client. Such things unfortunately happen from time to time, whatever the counsellor's therapeutic orientation, and therapist abuse of clients must largely stem from unresolved counter-transference feelings in this negative sense.

Counter-transference also refers to those feelings that the counsellor experiences which can enhance empathy with and understanding of the client. Sometimes, for instance, a counsellor can feel so irritated by a client that, were this not counselling, it would be tempting to break off the relationship. The client describes how difficult it is to sustain relationships, and the counsellor thinks: 'I'm not surprised!' But the counsellor does not stop there, but instead notes this personal reaction, and recognises that it perhaps helps identify what other people feel in the presence of this client. The counsellor may go even further, and wonder whether what people experience with the client can provide any clues as to what the client feels about her- or himself.

Another example of using the counsellor's feelings as they may be evoked by the client can be seen in a situation where he or she listens to a client's story, and feels angry at the way the client has been treated. Yet the counsellor is also aware that the client is not visibly moved, and even denies any feeling of being angry. Because the counsellor is able to identify with the client's situation, he or she experiences a feeling which the client may be afraid to admit and express. What is essential in all these examples is that a counsellor clarifies whether his or her feelings are being evoked by the client, or whether their source lies in the counsellor's own agenda. The close link between these two ways of understanding counter-transference is seen also in the way, even if a counsellor identifies particular thoughts and feelings as being more the counsellor's than the client's, he or she may still wonder why those feelings are appearing now? Could they in turn be saying that here is an area where client and counsellor impinge on each other? This too may lead, without confusing the boundaries between self and the other, to deeper understanding of the client. Suppose, for example, that a counsellor feels absolutely useless, and that he or she is of no help to the client. The counsellor does not know what to say or do to help the situation. This may be troubling to the trainee counsellor, or even to the therapist who looks too keenly for results. But even then, such a feeling in the counsellor might also be a reflection of the client's own feelings of helplessness.

In psychodynamic counselling, therefore, a counsellor pays special attention to inner feelings and associations. What the counsellor experiences at different moments often has as much to tell him or her as those things which the client is overtly expressing. The counsellor's counter-transference always has the potentiality for enhancing counselling, since it suggests possibilities which might not be obvious from the client's overt verbal and non-verbal communication.

THE REPARATIVE RELATIONSHIP

Clarkson has introduced two further dimensions to the therapeutic relationship which fully deserve attention. Neither are new, but each one makes explicit aspects of the relationship which hitherto have only been hinted at, or mentioned in passing.

Clarkson defines the reparative or developmentally needed relationship as the 'intentional provision by the psychotherapist of a corrective, reparative or replenishing relationship or action where the original parenting was deficient, abusive or over-protective' (1995: 108). This might appear to conflict with the quotation from Winnicott in Chapter 1, that the therapist 'can never make up to clients for what they have suffered in the past, but what he can do is to repeat the failure to love them enough . . . and then share with them and help them work through their feelings about his failure' (Malan, 1979: 141).

Yet we know that Winnicott wrote extensively about the facilitating environment which the therapist provides for the client; and from Guntrip's description of his analysis with Winnicott, we also know that Winnicott, in the very first session, said that he needed to respond to Guntrip, otherwise he would become like the mother who was unable to respond to the young Guntrip because of her distress (Guntrip, 1975). Guntrip himself quotes Winnicott that 'it is the mother–infant couple that can teach us the basic principles on which we base our therapeutic work' (Guntrip, 1968: 361).

So although it remains true that therapists and counsellors cannot remove the past, there is plenty of evidence that what they intend is in various ways to provide opportunities for clients to grow, to experience, to re-negotiate and in some respects even to re-live past experiences 'but with a new ending' (Alexander and French, 1946). Psychoanalysis may have tended to downplay the significance of the reparative relationship, through a defensive and envious attitude towards humanistic therapy, with its more positive estimation of the power of therapy and counselling to effect real change, which runs counter to the generally more pessimistic (or perhaps realistic?) Freudian view that beneath the veneer of civilisation we remain savage and cruel, and almost impossible to change radically. Yet Freud talked of cure by love, even if Lomas, writing tongue in cheek, suggests that therapists are too modest to claim that a patient can be helped by 'warmth, integrity, courage, strength, sensitivity, realism, honesty', preferring to say instead 'It's the technique' (Lomas, 1973: 135).

There is little doubt that the provision of a reliable, non-judgmental, non-retributive, listening, caring counsellor is a deliberate provision of a relationship which may not have been so obvious to the client in the family of origin, or in other situations: not so obvious, because clients sometimes remember the failures of parents more than their support, their criticism more than their love. Sometimes we have little way of knowing what early relationships were like in their totality. But there are also many clients whose histories have clearly been appalling, and they have been left terrified and suspicious of allowing anyone close. A psychodynamic counsellor need not lose what he or she believes is a more realistic view of human nature, that it can be selfish and cruel, when offering as he or she does a therapeutic environment in which there is some hope of change for the better. Even the important recognition in psychodynamic practice of the inevitability of failure, that the counsellor can never give or be all that the client wants, is not diluted by accepting the value of the reparative relationship. Indeed, it could be said that what makes counselling and therapy different is that any failure in the therapist can be talked about, and all manner of feelings expressed as a result of it, without resorting to shame, blame or rejection. That is in itself different from many of the failures which clients have experienced in the past. The willingness to work on the failure of the relationship makes it truly reparative.

TRANSCENDING DEFINITIONS

The complexity of this chapter's description of the therapeutic relationship may reinforce that view that psychodynamic counselling, like its mentor psychoanalytic psychotherapy, is full of intellectualising theory and technical terminology. Clearly I hope that it does not, and that the essential meeting of two people, one called counsellor and the other called client, is not lost sight of in the process of recognising the usefulness of understanding the different factors of their relationship.

It may initially appear that psychodynamic theory and practice has no obvious place for the fifth element of Clarkson's five-relationship framework. (The reader may have noted that in this chapter my own framework has so far included six styles of relating, and that this section embarks upon a seventh.) She describes the fifth element as the 'transpersonal relationship' and defines this as 'the timeless facet of the psychotherapeutic relationship, which is impossible to describe, but refers to the spiritual dimension of the healing relationship' (Clarkson, 1995: 181).

Whatever her analytic origins, this is not an auspicious start: 'impossible to describe' on the one hand, and 'spiritual' – hardly a concept which Freudians or Kleinians have much time for, even if Jungians give significant attention to the spiritual and the transpersonal, especially in the concept of the individuation process (Fordham, F., 1953). Yet there is a relevant concept here, of which there are glimpses in psychoanalytic literature.

We have to be careful not to confuse the transpersonal relationship with that deep intuitive meeting of persons which can take place inside and outside the therapeutic relationship, those moments when client and counsellor seem to have an understanding that is not easily described in words, but may be similar to deep intuition, identification or projective identification. But even having recognised that possibility there remains in psychoanalytic writing a recognition that there is so much more that the therapist does not understand, and indeed should not strain to understand. Winnicott touches on it when he writes: 'I suggest that in health there is a core to the personality that corresponds to the true self of the split personality: I suggest that this core never communicates with the world of perceived objects, and that the individual person knows that it must never be communicated with or influenced by external reality' (1965: 187). Bion appears to echo what Carl Rogers has said about needing to empty himself of pre-conceptions about a client, when Bion writes about the desirability of the state of 'NO memory, no desire, understanding' (1970: 129, his emphasis). Winnicott, again, wrote, 'All my life I have been imprisoned, frustrated, dogged by common-sense, reason, memories, desires and – the greatest bug-bear of all – understanding and being understood' (1971; quoted by Eigen, 1998: 16).

Such samples of cutting-edge thinking in some of the most important psychoanalytic writers contrast with the apparent idealisation of rationality, and the bid to understand as much as possible that is evidenced in Freud's great work, or the wish to relate everything in a harmonious whole evidenced in Jung's encyclopaedic accumulation of world literature, myth and culture. I think myself that Freud could be modest, and admit he was mistaken, even if at times he was forced by temperament and internal politics into a type of Mosaic leadership of a movement which has too often thought of itself in therapeutic terms as the chosen people. In all the vast literature on psychoanalytic and psychodynamic therapy it is vital to accept that there is so much more we do not know, or about which there is always doubt.

The interest in religion and spirituality is more apparent in psychoanalytic and psychodynamic thinking than it was in its more obviously atheistic period (Eigen, 1998; Jacobs, 1993a and b; Symington, 1994). Its relevance to the centrality of the therapeutic relationship lies in this: not in any claim by the counsellor and therapist to be able to cultivate a direct line to the transpersonal, or to seek mystical experience in the work with the client. Rather, it is a developing feature of the experienced therapist and counsellor that they feel at ease with a level of 'not-knowing', perhaps even of 'un-knowing', which in turn means that they do not anxiously seek for explanations, interpretations, links, identification of defences or any of these different aspects of the therapeutic relationship, but that they are open to unconscious communication, if and as and when it should yield hunches, flashes of inspiration, or the wisdom of the mundane. This is, I believe, a truly difficult state to achieve, given all the pressures of the work. It cannot be made to occur. It cannot be deliberately sought. Its absence does not invalidate anything that a psychodynamic counsellor tries to achieve. But its presence is a bonus of real worth.

THE COUNSELLING RELATIONSHIP IN ACTION

In her fourth session, Hannah had been able to overcome her resistance to telling me about her grandfather's night-time entry into her bedroom, and in the fifth we explored the threat this had presented to her because of its sexual implications. We spent several sessions in which this theme returned, and we worked together on the anger she felt at the way in which her grandfather had treated her as a replacement for his dead wife and his dead daughter. As the anger began to wane, she looked more depressed – the mood which had originally taken her to her doctor. I felt, however, that this feeling was deeper than she had experienced before, and was caused by a more far-reaching sense of loss than that occasioned either by the eviction from their London home, or by the experience of her grandfather stealing from her handbag.

The depth of sadness emerged in the session I now report. It illustrated the way in which the different components of the counsellor–client relationship could be seen at work:

'I feel very distant today,' she began; 'I don't know whether you'll understand. You're probably thinking about your holiday.'

I was indeed going on holiday, although I was not thinking about that at the time. I had previously told Hannah that there would be a break in our meetings in a month's time, and she had correctly assumed that a summer break meant that I would be going away. Her reference was to a real event. The feelings about not meeting which she might be experiencing were partly to be expected, because we had made a sufficiently strong relationship for a break to feel significant.

'Of course, I will be distant then', I replied, affirming first of all the reality of my holiday and of the break, 'but you seem to feel I am distant already, that I'm not fully here with you?'

I invited her to reflect on her opening words. I did not want to say too much, but rather to see whether she could make a link between her distant feeling and the way she presumed that I was already far away in my thoughts. Hannah pondered for a while, and then replied:

'No, I don't think it's about that. I don't know what it is.' She stopped, and appeared to think further about the situation. Here was an example of the working relationship, in which her own thinking and contributions were as important as mine.

After a few moments of silence, Hannah shook herself out of her thoughts, and said more. She told me about a woman who worked in the same office as her, who had shown her considerable kindness when she was settling into the new job. The woman was about the same age as Hannah, and lived alone. She had told her recently that her younger sister, whom she had not seen for a few months, was coming to stay with her. After work Hannah had gone to the bus terminus on her way home, and had seen this woman in the distance, obviously meeting her sister from the express coach. She described watching them hug each other, and how happy they both appeared to be; how they had gone arm-in-arm to another part of the terminus, out of Hannah's sight.

What she had witnessed remained with her all that weekend. She had found herself thinking about the older sister, imagining that she must have a lonely life, much as her own, but that there had been comfort for the two sisters when they had been reunited at the coach station. Thinking about the two of them, and the pleasure their weekend must be giving them both, she sometimes felt a sense of deep delight for them; but at other times she experienced an equally deep sadness. She felt a sense of resignation about the past and about her present circumstances, and a feeling of gradual separation between herself and the old man, her grandfather.

'What he has done has come between us', she sighed, 'but even if he hadn't there's something missing between us which he'll never understand.'

'And you feel I can't either', I suggested, recalling the opening words of the session, and clarifying the possible transference link between her grandfather and myself.

'Oh, you try', Hannah said, again showing her perception of the working relationship between us, 'but you can't be a sister to me; and that's what I felt I wanted when I saw the two of them together. I wanted someone who would hug me, hold me in her arms, someone who would look after me too, as she did . . .' Hannah's voice tailed off, choking a little, before she fell silent.

I was reminded at this point of a feeling which had come over me when I had seen her for the first time, although now she had put forward that same feeling in her own words. I had, as the reader might recall, sensed a wish on my own part to offer some physical comfort to Hannah. That 'counter-transference' feeling during the first session might have been my own transference, my wish to make things better rather than have to sit by helplessly while my client was upset. Perhaps offering comfort may have been a reparative gesture, something which Hannah needed, although I have already indicated (Chapter 2), that this would be an unusual step for a psychodynamic counsellor to take. In this instance, even in this fifth session, such a move would, I suspect, have been potentially threatening to Hannah, rather than reparative. But I was interested that while I had not acted upon it, I had not felt able at that time to discriminate the source of my feeling: was it just my own difficulty (counter-transference)? or part of a therapeutic stance (reparative)? or was I indeed picking up part of Hannah's problem (a different form of counter-transference)? This present session was different, because the feeling I had initially experienced clearly fitted with her own words about her wish that she might be hugged, held and looked after – but by a woman, not a man. What I thought I was picking up was an example of maternal transference. It seemed the right time to make a transference interpretation.

I waited until Hannah looked up at me, perhaps wanting me to speak. 'There is something very important here, which I might be able to understand, although I can't take away the loneliness of your feeling. The reason I can't help, and your grandfather can't help, may be because we are men; but I think you are not just looking for a sister. As you have lost faith in your grandfather, you have become more aware of how much you miss not having had a real mother. Your grandfather has missed your mother too, but to him *you* have been a substitute for her. But *he* has never been able to replace the woman you lost. And I think my going away on holiday is making you feel that I'm not a good substitute mother either.'

There was much more that might have been said, some of which we were able to look at during the session, and some of which came up in a later session before the break. The younger sister whom she had seen at the coach terminus was also coming on holiday. Holidays meant members of a family spending time together. It also seemed to mean being re-united with those whom you have not seen for a long time. The woman in the office was having a holiday weekend, and I was having a holiday myself. Hannah was not able to have a holiday, and this emphasised her feelings of being distant from members of her own family. She had felt many things when she had seen the two sisters together, including, as it turned out, some envy of their relationship. When the woman had shown kindness to her at work, Hannah had felt rather special, but when she saw the way the woman greeted her younger sister, Hannah realised that she was no more special than anyone else. She felt jealous. The 'holiday week-end' that the two sisters had also contributed to Hannah's feeling 'distant'. So, too, my approaching holiday made her feel distant from me, and aware that in reality I had a family, to which she did not belong.

There were all these possibilities in what Hannah told me. I only concentrated in this session upon one of them, the distance between us which my holiday caused, and my distance repeating the failure in her own mothering. It is quite usual for only one transference interpretation to be made in a session, and for the implications of it to be explored both then and in subsequent sessions, as long as the client's response confirms the value of the interpretation. Working through an important transference insight can take many months. But in allowing Hannah to voice her reactions to my letting her down, and about my distance, I was giving her the chance to value the validity of her own feelings (the reparative relationship).

If the transference relationship has (as it certainly does) a special place in psychodynamic counselling, 'in action' interpretations of it are made carefully, and with due regard for the proper distinction between what is a normal relationship between two human beings, and what is carried into the relationship from past and external situations. Without the other aspects of the counsellor–client relationship described in this chapter, use of transference alone easily becomes a game which is played with the client. Yet without it, psychodynamic counsellors are deprived of a valuable means of re-experiencing the ghosts of old relationships in the 'here and now'. Gradually some of those ghosts can be laid to rest as new, less transferential and more realistic perceptions of the counsellor and others are translated back into the client's other relationships and internal world.

My approaching holiday helped Hannah and me look at some of the ghosts in her inner world. It also rehearsed the termination of the counselling relationship. In the final chapter we see how endings in connection with counselling repeat earlier experiences of loss.

7

Breaks and Endings

Hannah Ends Counselling

It was the first session after the two-week break. Hannah arrived early, and when I met her in the waiting-room she looked relieved to see me. 'Did you have a nice time?', she asked, as she sat down. I nodded in reply to her question, but did not want to be drawn into talking about my holiday. I asked her how she had felt while I was away.

'It's been all right,' she replied, but without much life in the words. If anything, there was an edge in her voice, which made me wonder what she really felt. 'I think we're going to have to move.'

This remark dropped like a bombshell, and threw me off-balance. Was she reacting to my break so strongly that she wanted to leave counselling? Was this a way of turning the tables on me for leaving her? This was a possibility, although it was out of character for Hannah, who, if anything, had so far in her life remained far too loyal to those around her, and had tended to put herself last. Nevertheless, some clients do react to the counsellor's absence by missing sessions themselves, or even breaking off counselling earlier than initially agreed. I needed more information. 'You're going to have to move?', I repeated, inviting Hannah to expand upon her remark.

Hannah found it difficult to relate what had been happening in the two weeks I had been away since she was clearly distressed by events. Her grandfather had been out several afternoons when she had returned from work; at first she had thought nothing of it, but she had found some betting slips, and guessed that he had started gambling again. She had tackled him about it, and there had been a row between them – she had for once spoken up, and been prepared to show her anger. But she was clearly not convinced that bringing the issue into the open had altered anything, and the next day her grandfather had arrived home even later, accompanied by another (younger man), whom Hannah could only describe as 'exceedingly shady'. 'I can see it all,' she concluded, 'he's going to let us down again.'

There were obviously some real issues here, and I did not want to lose sight of them. At the same time, I felt that my absence had made the situation more difficult for Hannah. 'I wonder whether you feel that I too have let you down, by being away at a time when you perhaps needed my support?'

'Well, I must confess, that I felt really angry with you for going off enjoying yourself, and leaving me to cope with all this. I think it was feeling angry with you that made me decide to have it out with Grandpa – it was just bottling up inside of me.'

'And now you feel you have to go away? You want to leave him?'

I had misheard her intention. 'No, I can't leave him, he doesn't know what he's doing. I'm frightened if we stay here that he'll get into real trouble. We shall just have to move, just get out, I don't know where.'

The desperation in her voice indicated that she had not really thought out such a decision, and was throwing everything away in the vain hope that by moving on she might escape the problems. There were thankfully some signs that she had been able to speak her mind to the old man, even if his reaction appeared to have been to find an 'ally' to bring home with him. I tried putting it to Hannah that staying meant a job, and somewhere to live, and would allow her to go on seeing me. Perhaps we could even look into getting some help for the old man. I still felt that, realistic though her situation was, my own break had exacerbated her reaction.

The more I tried to reason, the greater the panic Hannah showed. She was determined to move, and I was not going to stand in her way. She said that this would be the last session: 'You men are all the same, trying to push me around. You think I'm just dumb.'

'I think you're angry with me, because you think I'm trying to hold on to you. You think I'm more concerned about myself than about you. By going away last week, and indeed with the ending coming up in July you feel I control everything; and that what you want doesn't matter. It is important for you to take control, but I wonder whether you are choosing to get away from me because it's easier than controlling or breaking free from the old man?'

There was a certain desperation in me too, which led to my making a somewhat 'blunderbuss' interpretation – a wide spray of ideas, one of which I hoped might strike home. I did not think running away was the solution, yet I did not want to come over as another of the dominating males Hannah so readily saw around her. I was not sure which of my remarks, if any, had actually helped, but she calmed down, and said she would come just one more week, 'if they were still around'.

I was grateful for this, because at least it would allow us to use the time to pull together our work over the ten sessions, and look at what, if anything, had changed for her; at what still troubled her; at how she felt counselling had helped; and in what respects counselling had disappointed her. Unfortunately, the sudden termination of her counselling was not to give me the opportunity to work through the ending as thoroughly as I would have liked. There was, however, a chance that her wish to move was linked with feelings of being let down by my own absence, and that this last session had helped her to recognise this. In that case Hannah might change her mind, and decide to stay with the original contract which, by now, I was feeling could usefully be reviewed and renewed.

Either I had not sufficiently anticipated the strength of her reaction to the break, or the new external circumstances in which she found herself were too difficult to tolerate, even with the help of counselling. Hannah, when she returned the following week, said that they were definitely leaving the area, and she would look for work in another part of the country. They would be going at the weekend. I used the last session to consider whether Hannah felt any difference between herself as she was now, and herself as she had been when she had first visited her doctor. As I have recorded earlier (in the summary on her case-notes, p. 62), Hannah said that she felt less depressed, and I was able to point out that she had confronted her grandfather with some of her angry feelings. She said, smiling, that I had not 'turned out to be as bad as I first thought you'd be', and 'perhaps there are some people in this life who aren't out just for what they can get'.

Nevertheless, I suggested to her that she still felt let down by my inability to show her enough of the care and love which she had missed out upon as a child, and which had come home to her during the last few years. Despite our ability to work together, I suspected that she was still suspicious of any relationship which evoked the wish for closeness that she wanted and yet feared. Perhaps she wanted to ensure that I would not let her down any further by making the break herself.

145

I kept to myself my own hunch that there was still a lot of grief buried deep in her at the loss of her mother, and of the closeness of mother and child; and I did not comment on another area which she had alluded to in a session before the break, when Hannah had said all the women in her family died young. What I had suggested on that occasion was that perhaps our meetings were arranged to end at a point when it might feel as if our relationship was still only at a young stage. But I felt some concern in that particular session, and again, as we finished, that the fruitless search for mother which her moving around the country suggested, and her inability to break free of her grandfather, might even make death a tempting escape from everything that oppressed her.

Hannah asked me whether she could get in touch with me when she knew where she was going to be, so that I could suggest a counsellor in the area. I said that this was possible, and that I thought it would be helpful to find someone who could see her for longer than I had done. I was a little dubious about my last remark, because it seemed afterwards like veiled criticism of her for leaving me early. On the other hand, I felt that Hannah now needed the opportunity of longer-term counselling or therapy, to work on some of the other issues which she had begun to identify.

I felt sad to see her go – it had felt a useful piece of brief counselling which had met some of the aims I had set out in my early notes (see p. 58). It had lightly touched on some of the other goals, even though Hannah had terminated before we had the chance to look at them further. I had a brief letter the following month to say that they were in a large city about fifty miles away, and that she 'hated' it. This was followed by a picture-postcard another six weeks later, in which she said they had settled in a quiet village, where she had found work as a housekeeper, and grandfather as a jobbing gardener. The short sentences concluded: 'A quiet place at last. Grandpa depressed and clinging, and very tiring. But we look forward to the spring.' I did not hear from her again.

THE SIGNIFICANCE OF THE BREAK

The ending with Hannah, in many ways unsatisfactory because of its surprise, and because of the issues it left unresolved, is not untypical of some counselling. There is some progress, and therefore a sense of achievement for the client and for the counsellor, but much remains which might have been worked through given more time. However, even psychodynamic work at its most intense and lengthy, as seen in psychoanalysis itself, inevitably has to leave loose ends. Freud himself debated whether analysis can ever be completed in one of his last papers *Analysis Terminable and Interminable* (1937).

If psychoanalysis, psychotherapy, or counselling is, in theory, never-ending, since there is always more to be learned about oneself, in practice it is certainly limited: by time, by the skills of the therapist or counsellor, and by the defences in the client. Although this may sound a truism, this situation reflects life itself, in the course of which many people experience less than satisfactory endings to relationships. Everyone experiences, at some time or other, endings and losses, where there are unresolved feelings. There are so many losses, endings and new beginnings in the course of personal growth and development that it would be surprising if some at least were not handled satisfactorily. From birth itself, through the frequent changes that take place in the parent–child relationship in response to the child's growth and development, and right through to the changes and chances of adult life, everyone passes through a series of transitions. Some of these are major upheavals, and recognised as particular points of stress.

I need not elaborate these ends and the beginnings, or those little deaths which provide us with hints of our own mortality. It is sufficient to be reminded of some of the losses which had proved difficult for the two clients I have been describing in this book: loss of mother, and eviction from home (Hannah); loss of freedom and job, of wife, of the companionship of others, separation from his daughter and then loss of her when she married, and leaving his 'mother' country (Karl). This is only to list actual events, and not to include other more subtle losses, such as the loss of trust which Hannah experienced when her grandfather stole from her purse, or Karl's partial loss of control over his own life when he agreed to make a contract to meet with me.

These types of loss give rise to many of the difficulties and negative feelings which people in general experience, so that it is often losses and the accompanying feelings that lie at the root of difficulties clients present when coming for counselling. The psychodynamic approach concentrates much more upon helping the client to work through these negative experiences than it does upon encouraging and underlining the client's positive experiences, although this latter aspect is not neglected. As I made clear in the opening chapter, the psychodynamic counsellor is concerned to help the client recognise that the counsellor cannot make up for past losses, so the feelings of disappointment, anger, sadness and other emotions that are evoked by such disappointment can be expressed more openly. The psychodynamic approach does not think it is sufficient to provide a warm and facilitative environment in the hope that this alone will be enough to help the client overcome obstacles to development and growth: such an environment is necessary, may be very important from a developmental point of view, but it is not often sufficient in those instances where disappointment and distress run very deep. Whereas person-centred counselling (and some other humanistic therapies) perhaps puts considerable stress upon love, psychodynamic counselling concentrates equally on anger and hate, and the other negative feelings which arise from separation and loss. Through the counselling relationship, disappointments and losses that have led to negative feelings can be re-experienced; and the client can discover that negative feelings need neither undermine relationships, nor destroy more positive feelings.

The psychodynamic counsellor therefore takes opportunities, when they occur, to show the client that he or she (the counsellor) is in part repeating some of the failures and disappointments which the client in some way experienced as a child in relation to her or his parents. Many of these opportunities to demonstrate such links come from the breaks in counselling, as well as disappointments in the therapeutic relationship. For example, the end of the session means that the counsellor imposes time limits; regularly spaced appointments mean that the counsellor is not on 'stand-by', or 'on tap' whenever the client needs the counsellor; the counsellor's (and to a lesser extent the client's) holidays force the client to go without the counsellor for a longer time than usual; and terminating the relationship throws up many feelings about the counsellor, about counselling, and about having to cope on one's own. In fact, every break in the continuity of the sessions has the potentiality of providing a rehearsal for the termination of the contract. At the same time everything which is experienced in relation to the losses in counselling and of the counsellor, acts as a way of opening up old wounds and, perhaps for the first time, allowing them to heal.

In fact, just as there are events in life which are clear losses, and there are more subtle losses that are often connected with those events, so in counselling the actual breaks and termination provide only one way of looking at loss. There are more subtle losses in the counselling process which the client has to face in order to enter it, and remain within it. Wolff (1977), in a paper on loss as a central theme in psychotherapy, points out that in therapy (and by implication in psychodynamic counselling) certain beliefs and illusions have to be given up in order to prepare the way for new beginnings. He includes the loss of belief that one is independent and can cope on one's own, the loss of face that may accompany entering counselling or owning and sharing less acceptable parts of oneself. Likewise, the person who comes for counselling often has to give up out-of-date values, as well as face the fear that renouncing old attitudes may lead to uninhibited licence and lack of control. Other aspects which involve loss in counselling include giving up infantile wishes that cannot be sustained in adult life – for example, the desire for a life of perfect bliss which is never marred by sorrow or disappointment. Illusions have to be given up in order to face the reality of life.

Wolff concludes his paper by looking at loss as experienced in relationships to the therapist. The psychodynamic counsellor can usefully note his examples, since they link to the significance of breaks and endings. While the counsellor tries to be reliable, and provide regular continuity, the client has to accept the disappointment that the counsellor cannot be a personal friend, or parent figure, and that the counsellor is only available to her or him for a particular span of time, both in the session, and for the duration of the contract. Similarly, although the counsellor tries to practise his or her expertise as sensitively and as skilfully as possible, the counsellor will always fall short of the ideal, and will fail the client by not listening, by not understanding, or by making the wrong interpretation. None of this needs spell disaster (providing the counsellor is not afraid to bring these losses and disappointments into the open), because such frustrations present the client with the opportunity of learning to cope with the disappointments that are generally inevitable in life.

As counselling approaches the point when counsellor and client have agreed to finish, these disappointments combine with different feelings of loss which are bound to be experienced in one form or another, and which are described below. The main features that occur in the course of separation and mourning (Bowlby, 1973, 1980; Kübler-Ross, 1970; Parkes, 1972) are also to some degree present in the counsellor–client relationship. How strongly these are felt depends on how much of themselves clients have invested in the process, and upon just how strong their feelings are (both positive and negative) towards the counsellor. Here again, the termination of counselling often re-awakens earlier feelings and fantasies that may either be remembered, or may have been repressed as too painful to bear. The counsellor listens for evidence of such feelings, and tries to help them to be expressed, particularly as the end of counselling approaches. The recognition of such feelings may make all the difference between a clean break (where the client can separate satisfactorily from the counsellor) and a messy ending. In the latter case, the client adopts different strategies to try to hang on to the counsellor, maintaining contact, wanting extra sessions, or (in the worst handled endings) actually having to go to a second counsellor in order to resolve the unfinished issues left over from the first.

HANDLING BREAKS AND TERMINATION

The termination of counselling is thus very important. So too are breaks for holidays, or gaps in the regularity of sessions, caused by the absence of the counsellor, or the absence of the client, if the client is prevented from attending due to circumstances beyond her or his control. A well-handled termination provides an opportunity for counselling to be brought to a close in a way which respects the client's feelings, as well as providing an opening for earlier losses to be re-lived. If breaks in counselling seem less important, they are nonetheless, as I have observed above, a rehearsal for the end of counselling, a brief foretaste of what it will then be like not to be able to see the counsellor. Yet for some clients, particularly those who rely heavily upon their counsellor, even the absence caused by a single missed session can be experienced as severely discomforting and frightening.

If the opportunities to use the experience of endings are to be maximised, the psychodynamic counsellor needs to prepare the client for any alteration in the arrangements. It is partly out of respect for the client, therefore, that a counsellor will ensure that any planned break is communicated to the client at least three weeks before it is due to occur. This is also to permit the client to experience what the impending break feels like. To that end a psychodynamic counsellor listens especially carefully for references to separation, loss or ending in what the client is saying when a break has been notified. References to outside losses may be displaced descriptions (see Chapter 5) of feelings which the client is also experiencing in relation to the counsellor.

For example, two weeks before we had planned to finish, Karl was telling me about the news of his release from prison, and how it had given rise in him to a curious mixture of relief that he would be free, but also of dread of how he would cope in the world outside. I thought that Karl might also be referring to counselling coming to an end. On the one hand, ending might be a relief, because he dreaded being confined by a regular arrangement. Yet it could also be causing him some concern as to how well he would cope, when he could no longer see me, with those occasional, terrifying episodes he had. I asked him, therefore, 'Is that perhaps how you feel about us stopping in two weeks' time?' Karl replied that he was a little worried about it; and I then added the other side of his feelings: 'And perhaps a feeling of freedom too, at not having to come here?' Karl smiled at that, and shook his head, leaving me wondering whether the smile meant I was right, or whether the shaking of his head meant I was wrong.

Even if there are no references in what clients say which suggest that the break or the ending has some significance for them, the counsellor continues to remind clients that there are 'three weeks', 'two weeks', and 'one week' to go, always keeping that event to the forefront, putting it on the agenda for clients to pick up as they wish. If nothing is forthcoming, it is often helpful to ask the client what he or she feels about the break. It is sometimes only then that the client surprises the counsellor by saying something like 'I shall miss this'; although there will be other clients who deny the break means anything at all to them. Even the denial of feelings might be interesting, especially when, for instance, it is made by those who cannot allow feelings for anyone to impinge upon them.

Similarly, after a break a psychodynamic approach means that the counsellor listens out for references that might point to the client's feelings during and about the break. This applies whether or not the break was intentional. Indeed, it is even more important to listen for the client's response to any unforeseen absence either on the part of the counsellor or the client. Again, these references might be oblique ones, the 'displacement' of feelings outside the session, that belong just as much unconsciously to the counselling relationship as they do consciously to any outside events or persons that the client is describing.

Hannah, for example, in the session at the start of this chapter, spoke of her anger with her grandfather, and I used that as an opportunity to relate what she was saying to her feelings about me and my holiday. Hannah confirmed that she had indeed felt that I had gone off and enjoyed myself, leaving her to cope on her own; and this was very similar to the feeling which she had about her grandfather going off and enjoying himself by gambling, leaving her to take all the responsibility for managing their home.

The first session after the break is especially valuable as a time to look for the client's reactions, although in some instances those feelings may continue into later sessions. Prior to the break, and immediately afterwards, the counsellor therefore pays special attention to anything which appears to refer to that event. This does not mean that the reality of the external situations which the client describes is denied or neglected by the counsellor, but that wherever possible the counsellor looks for possible links between what is happening within the counselling relationship and what has been experienced elsewhere. Using the 'triangle of insight' referred to in the last chapter, the counsellor might be able to demonstrate parallels between a client's feelings about breaks and endings in the 'here and now', and in past relationships.

An inadequately handled break, or an unplanned break (which by definition means that it cannot be anticipated) can often be rescued once the sessions resume, particularly by drawing out the negative feelings which the client may have towards the counsellor. I thought I might have handled the break badly in Hannah's case, and was therefore anxious that her decision to move on was not 'acting out' (see pp. 71, 108) her discontent with me.

However, following the termination of counselling, no such opportunity exists for the client to share feelings about the final break from the counsellor. The client who asks for further sessions after the end of counselling might do so because the ending has not been sufficiently worked through. (Of course, some clients ask for more sessions because new circumstances threaten their equilibrium.) Therefore, as termination approaches, the focus of the counsellor's work is upon the client's experience of the loss of these sessions. If the contract negotiated is a short one, ending is in sight from the very start, and a counsellor might therefore use any opportunities that present themselves to observe the frustration of the limits set upon the client. Longer contracts, or those which are open-ended (where there is no definite limit set at the start of counselling), need either a reminder or actual negotiation of the end.

Negotiation of a date to finish should take into account how long counselling has been going on. Thus counselling which has lasted for twenty weeks ideally requires the ending to be negotiated (or focused upon) ten weeks before it is due to take place. Counselling which has continued for a year ideally requires three months' notice of ending. With particularly dependent clients it is no exaggeration to suggest that it might be important to work with the prospect of ending from the first session of counselling. If a counsellor makes a contract to meet weekly for six months with a client who has a history of being dependent in her or his relationships, and of being unable to let people go, the counsellor will need, as each week goes by, to take up references to the end of the counselling relationship with continual reminders to the client of the 'dead-line', and of all that it might mean.

Furthermore, even if the counsellor is referring a client to another source of help, the ending with him or her is just as important as when the client is ceasing counselling altogether. A badly handled ending (whether the client has seen the counsellor for two sessions or two years) can present innumerable difficulties to the counsellor or therapist to whom the client is referred, even to the point of deterring the client from taking up the help offered.

The Counsellor's Feelings about Endings

If breaks and terminations are to be handled well, counsellors need to acknowledge their own feelings, especially those which are often obscured by their own difficulties (or their 'counter-transference' – see Chapter 6). Their own relief at having a break (especially if the demands on them are intense) can prevent them from understanding what such a break means for their clients. A few clients will regard the counsellor's holiday as an unnecessary indulgence – resentful, for example, that the counsellor can take a rest when they themselves experience no relief from their troublesome feelings or situations. Again, when a counsellor finishes with one client, there is normally another person waiting to take over that slot, so that a counsellor's 'need to be needed' is soon met. However important the individual client is, most of them are fairly quickly filed in the counsellor's memory as soon as the new client arrives. So counsellors may not permit themselves to experience the sadness which their clients feel at the ending of what for them might be one of the most significant (and unusual) relationships they have ever had.

The desire of counsellors to be useful, and to feel that their work has been of help to their clients, can make it difficult for them to hear their clients' disappointment at what has not been achieved, even if some of the initial expectations were unrealistic or over-optimistic. If they cannot accept the anger or frustration which their clients sometimes experience at having to stop after so short a time, counsellors may also be unable to help clients to acknowledge negative feelings at the point of leaving. Furthermore, the lack of confidence or self-esteem in some counsellors can blind them to the immensely important position they hold in the eyes of some of their clients. Only when a counsellor has learned to acknowledge the whole range of feelings that are associated with separation and loss for her- or himself can clients be encouraged to face the positive and negative feelings which often emerge as counselling comes to an end.

FEELINGS ASSOCIATED WITH BREAKS AND TERMINATION

All the feelings that accompany loss and bereavement can be experienced in relation to the counsellor and counselling. Sadness at ending is the most obvious one, but it is seldom the only one present. A counsellor offers the client opportunities to reflect upon what he or she (the client) is experiencing as counselling comes to an end, but it is often necessary to draw out other emotions, which the client may not express, or might suppress. These can be tentatively suggested so that, even though the client may reject them, various feelings about ending will have been identified as appropriate responses. Some of them may indeed actually be experienced at a later date, and may then be less surprising to the client.

Let us take sadness as an example for the moment: some clients may reject the counsellor's suggestion that they (the clients) might be feeling sad at ending counselling, and indeed they are probably telling the truth when they refute such an emotion. At that point they mean what they say. They feel nothing in particular. On leaving the room for the last time, however, they may suddenly feel a lump in the throat, and a twinge of sadness. It is far better that the counsellor should have acknowledged this possibility beforehand, because then such clients can say to themselves, 'It's all right to feel sad. He obviously expected me to, otherwise he wouldn't have mentioned it.' Had the counsellor not mentioned the possibility of sadness, the clients who actually feel very low later may mistake their sadness for a return of the depression that first made them seek help.

It is for this reason that I suggest that it is important to test out various responses to endings over the last few weeks of counselling, whenever possible linking such interpretations of hidden feelings to similar material which the client has already presented. Careful listening and this ability to link references in the material to the counselling relationship both come with practice, especially when supervision provides the counsellor with the opportunity to reflect on the experience of termination.

There are, however, many more emotions than sadness at the end of counselling. Some of them may not occur when counselling has been brief, or when it has stayed on the level of external, current issues in the client's life. Yet even in short work there can be different feelings about the way in which counselling has gone. Relief at ending is possible, where a client had been unsure about coming to counselling, and had accepted it more out of a sense of duty or compliance than from a genuine desire to use it. Yet even the end of longer counselling with well-motivated clients may, in one sense, be viewed with some relief, because the sessions and the learning have in part been painful, however beneficial the end result.

Because counselling often tends to be shorter than psychotherapy, there can also be disappointment that the work that continued successfully cannot go on for longer. There may be gratitude for this chance to reflect, tinged with some sadness at its coming to an end; but it can take the form of much more angry feelings – feelings of being let down, of being manipulated by the counsellor into ending sooner than desired. Here the counsellor's control of the timing and even of the number of sessions needs to be acknowledged as contributing to some of the negative feelings that are present.

Disappointment, sadness, anger, and relief are the main feelings which the client may be helped to express. In longer counselling there may be some clients who deny any particular feeling about ending and such denial of feelings is probably a defence against ending. Understanding the defence against such feelings (see Chapter 5) is more important than questioning the client's denial. Other feelings which are also present include appreciation by clients of the help given to them by the counsellor, as well as some curiosity about what the counsellor thinks of them. It is not unusual for clients to expect that the counsellor will provide a final summary, which encapsulates his or her present understanding of the client. In doing this they may, of course, be looking for the counsellor's approval that they have been 'good clients' – a feeling that might be linked to concern about what parent-figures think of them. On the other hand, clients' wishes to assess how far they have come, in what direction they might go, and how they can integrate some of the changes and insights, are helpful ones to follow.

Here the psychodynamic counsellor (like the person-centred counsellor) avoids the temptation to become the expert. Indeed, in much counselling practice contact with the client is too brief for any more than a partial picture to be formed. It is better to invite clients who ask these questions to assess their own progress. In what ways have they changed? What new understanding have they acquired? What aspects of themselves do they still wish to change, or to go on thinking about within themselves? As I have already made clear above, counselling inevitably finishes with a series of incomplete answers. Partial change, fresh insight, and whole areas that remain largely unexplored will be the norm, as it was in Hannah's case.

In putting back the initiative and the responsibility to the clients, at the end of counselling as much as during it, the counsellor is confirming that clients can become their own observer and (in the best, non-judgmental, sense of the word) their own critic. What the psychodynamic counsellor tries to convey, throughout the course of counselling, is that the counsellor's function can be shared and ultimately taken over by the client's own central ego. Thus the counsellor's skills and expertise are translated, within the limitations imposed by time and by the readiness of the client, into an inner acceptance, into an ability to listen to the different 'voices' within oneself, into a facility for balancing the pressures coming from the different sides of the personality, into a critical facility for assessing thought and action, into interpretation and understanding of painful thoughts and feelings, and into the encouragement and enhancement of insight.

It is therefore the counsellor's hope that a client will come to regard her- or himself in the same way as the counsellor has done. In psychodynamic terms, as has been mentioned in earlier chapters, a process of internalisation takes place, wherein the client begins at first to talk within as if he or she were talking with the counsellor, and imagining the responses which the counsellor might make. Gradually, however, the internalisation becomes more complete, so that the central ego takes over from the counsellor, and the counsellor is no longer 'seen' or 'heard' as a separate person. Instead, the counsellor is experienced as another unconscious contributor to the client's internal world, alongside all those other significant persons who inhabit it, and who help constitute it.

The limitations imposed in some counselling settings often mean that a counsellor has to let a client go after a relatively short number of sessions, aware that much remains unsaid, and that new crises may well expose the same or different areas of vulnerability. Counselling may claim only modest success. Nevertheless, the ability to let the client go is itself a sign of good parenting. Counsellors who are over-concerned for their clients' future welfare and ability to cope tend to find themselves unable to handle endings, by deferring them, or by allowing the client (without good reason) to go on claiming more and more time.

Decisions about endings are not straightforward. One of the features of counselling is that it has to handle such decisions much more frequently than is the case with long-term psychotherapy. Nevertheless, Malan (1976), who has helped pioneer brief psychotherapy at the Tavistock Clinic in London (where time limits are an essential feature), argues that one of the key factors in the efficacy of brief therapy (by which he means about thirty sessions) is the ability of the therapist to interpret the significance of the ending to the patient. Time-limited work makes a virtue out of a necessity, by using the ending constructively to deepen the client's experience of coping with the universal reality of loss.

A REVEALING ENDING

I had arranged with Karl that we would meet for six weeks, when he himself wished to finish, just before his daughter's wedding. The reader may recall that he had shown considerable ambivalence about continuing to see me. I think my attempts to understand his resistance (his concern not to be controlled either by counselling or by the unconscious material that might emerge in counselling) helped Karl feel a little safer, and therefore he was able to come on time and make more use of the sessions.

I responded carefully to the material Karl produced, aware of the fear which he felt (and which I also shared given the brief time we would have to meet) that he could be overwhelmed by the terror that he experienced in the semi-dreamlike episodes he had gone through some mornings. I was content to let him control the content, and for my responses to be aimed at supporting the adaptations he was making to life in this country. Just over half-way through the contract, with three weeks to go before termination, Karl seemed more confident of his ability to cope. I reminded him of the date we had agreed to finish.

Karl looked a little anxious, and went quiet. After a few minutes' silence, and because he had a rather vacant expression, I intervened. 'What's on your mind? You seem far away,' I suggested. 'I've been robbed,' he mumbled.

He had used precisely those words at our first meeting. I did not know then what they meant, although I was reminded of them now. Having since then heard more of his story, I could see how he had been robbed when he had lost his freedom, his wife, and most of his daughter's childhood because of his imprisonment. But what made him use those words now? The mention of the break seemed to have triggered the phrase.

I was reluctant to interpret our relationship too obviously, although I felt strongly that reminding him of the end had somehow triggered the phrase about being robbed. 'You've said that before. Do you feel you are being robbed?' I brought the verb into the present tense, because whatever had happened in the past was being re-experienced in some way now.

'I'm frightened of that feeling: all I can see is darkness, the moon and the stars, a small window of pale light.' Again, some of the phrases he was using had appeared in our first meeting. Working on termination sometimes brings back some of the difficulties and symptoms which the client initially presents to the counsellor. It is like an indication that the client does not want to leave, and so reproduces the original concerns in order to hang on to the counsellor. But in this case we were returning to something which had not yet been looked at.

'What do those pictures in your mind mean to you?' I asked. Fortunately, we still had enough time in the session to explore his current experience, because I had introduced my reminder of termination early on.

'Prison,' replied Karl sadly. 'Prison – I remember looking out at night, at the vast space in the darkness, at the moon and the stars. Somehow I felt a softness in the light which I couldn't find anywhere else in that harsh place. I remember especially the sense of comfort the night sky gave me when I learned my wife had deserted me. . .'

Karl had been calm while he told me about the moon and stars, but a look of anguish pained him as he made the further connection to his wife. The rest of the session was tense, and I suggested he might prefer to meet for a few more weeks than we had originally agreed. I had the feeling that my reminder of the end of our sessions had brought something important to the surface.

During the next two weeks Karl elaborated on material he had already told me about in the sessions. It was not until the following week that the breakthrough came. It was the session following his daughter's wedding. Lucy and her husband had gone away for a few days, and Karl had experienced a massive recurrence of his states of reverie. In fact, the friend who had first suggested he see me called me to say how concerned he was about his state of mind.

Perhaps I had been slow to see it, and the reader has already anticipated the essential link between Karl's disturbing experiences and current events. As it was, it was only as he spoke about the importance of not letting Lucy know how he was – because he did not want to spoil the young couple's holiday – that I began to see the real significance of 'I've been robbed'. Much as he liked Lucy's husband, at a deeper level he felt that he was taking Lucy away from him: Lucy, who had been (in a sense) a guiding star; Lucy, the thought of whom had sustained him in the dark days of his imprisonment. The shifting states of mind, which so disturbed him because they threatened to take him back to those dreadful days, reminded him of the former loss of his wife; but on another level they seemed to repeat the experience of looking out to the freedom and comfort of the night sky, and so acted in some way to distract him from the loss which had become more real during the weeks before the wedding.

My reminder of the time that we had planned to end had in fact brought home to him the even greater proximity of Lucy's wedding. That was why he had reacted so strangely to it. However, had he not reacted in that way, he might not have given those few clues which, in the end, helped to form a more complete picture.

I told Karl that I had heard from his friend. Any communication such as that must be shared with the client. During that session we looked at what had happened to him over the last few days, and I suggested there might be a connection between his mental state and Lucy's wedding. Karl defended against this at first, vehemently asserting that he was only too pleased for her, and only wanted what was best for her. I had to wait until the next session before I could add that though he truly cared about her, he also cared so much for her that losing her was almost too hard to take. 'Indeed', I said, 'She means so much to you that there's a conflict in you between, on the one hand, letting her go and finding pleasure in seeing her become her own person, and on the other, holding on to her as the light of your life.' In the next session Karl, by now almost free of disturbing thoughts, said that perhaps Lucy's marriage, even though he liked her husband, was associated in his mind with his wife's leaving him for another man.

Despite the precariousness of Karl's mental condition when I first saw him, and the long-term difficulties with which his past experiences might have left him, counselling was able to help him because a clear focus, and an immediate 'crisis' emerged: the crisis, which (as it became clearer) provided the focus, was brought about by the 'loss' of his daughter through her marriage. Karl was struggling to 'let her go'. Consciously he had accepted that her happiness in future now lay with another man; but unconsciously he had felt great distress, which he could not express directly, whether to Lucy or to himself. Unlike Hannah's grandfather, he was able to work through the parent-child relationship with his daughter towards the more adult relationship which her marriage now required. Furthermore, this adaptation, which he had already accepted in his conscious mind, became more complete when, through counselling, the unconscious protest could be heard, understood, accepted, and left behind.

CONCLUSION

Having reached this point, at the end of this book, I find myself in a similar position to the counsellor who finds it impossible to summarise adequately the long and varied journey through which client and counsellor have come over the period of counselling. The reader has followed my descriptions and examples of the main considerations that govern the practice of the psychodynamic approach. I hope that I have helped the reader to understand that whatever else happens, by way of careful listening and accurate responding and through the relationship between counsellor and client, from first contact to final session, the psychodynamic approach involves one particular perspective. If I had to single out one feature which underpins all the method and theory that is explained in these pages, it is the quietly reflective but persistent question: 'What does it – this word, that action, this memory, that feeling, this aspect of our relationship, that symbol, this defence, that explanation – what does it mean?'

SUGGESTIONS FOR
FURTHER READING

There is so much written about psychoanalysis, about its different theories, about many technical issues, case-histories, as well as applied psychoanalysis in literary and film criticism, in psycho-history, in sociology, and in the context of other disciplines, that the reader has a wonderful choice. But such a vast library is also daunting, and the particular books listed immediately below are perhaps the best suggestions for the next steps the reader might take, until such time as the reader wishes to make use of the immense body of writing in psychodynamic and psychoanalytic therapy, which many psychodynamic counsellors use to develop their skills and understanding.

Bettelheim, B. (1983) *Freud and Man's Soul.* London: Chatto and Windus/Hogarth Press.
Brown, D. and Pedder, J. (1991) *Introduction to Psychotherapy* (2nd edition). London: Routledge/Tavistock.
Cashdan, S. (1988) *Object Relations Therapy: Using the Relationship.* New York: Norton.
Erikson, E. (1965) *Childhood and Society.* Harmondsworth: Penguin.
Gomez, L. (1996) *An Introduction to Object Relations.* London: Free Association Books.
Jacobs, M. (1992) *Sigmund Freud.* London: Sage Publications.
Jacobs, M. (1998) *The Presenting Past* (revised and enlarged edition). Buckingham: Open University Press.
Journal of Psychodynamic Counselling. London: Routledge.

Jung, C.G. (1967) *Memories, Dreams and Reflections*. London: Fontana Books.

Klein, J. (1987) *Our Need for Others and Its Roots in Infancy*. London: Routledge.

Malan, D.H. (1979) *Individual Psychotherapy and the Science of Psychodynamics*. London: Heinemann Medical.

McLoughlin, B. (1995) *Developing Psychodynamic Counselling*. London: Sage Publications.

Rycroft, C. (1972) *A Critical Dictionary of Psychoanalysis*. London: Penguin.

Samuels, A. (1985) *Jung and the Post-Jungians*. London: Routledge.

Schmidt Neven, R. (1997) *Emotional Milestones from Birth to Adulthood: a Psychodynamic Approach*. London: Jessica Kingsley.

Segal, J. (1992) *Melanie Klein*. London: Sage Publications.

Symington, N. (1988) *The Analytic Experience*. London: Free Association Press.

BIBLIOGRAPHY

Alexander, F. and French, T.M. (1946) *Psychoanalytic Therapy*. New York: Ronald Press.

Balint, M., Ornstein, P.H. and Balint, E. (1972) *Focal Psychotherapy: an Example of Applied Psychoanalysis*. London: Tavistock.

Bettelheim, B. (1983) *Freud and Man's Soul*. London: Chatto and Windus/Hogarth Press.

Bion, W.R. (1970) *Attention and Interpretation*. London: Karnac Books.

Bowlby, J. (1973) *Attachment and Loss*, Volume II: *Separation: Anxiety and Anger*. New York: Basic Books.

Bowlby, J. (1979) *The Making and Breaking of Affectional Bonds*. London: Tavistock.

Bowlby, J. (1980) *Attachment and Loss*, Volume III: *Loss: Sadness and Depression*. London: Hogarth Press.

Burnham, J.B. (1986) *Family Therapy*. London: Tavistock.

Clarkson, P. (1991) 'A multiplicity of therapeutic relationships', *British Journal of Psychotherapy*, 7 (2): 148–63.

Clarkson, P. (1994) 'The psychotherapeutic relationship', in P. Clarkson and M. Pokorny (eds), *The Handbook of Psychotherapy*. London: Routledge, pp. 28–48.

Clarkson, P. (1995) *The Therapeutic Relationship in Psychoanalysis, Counselling Psychology and Psychotherapy*. London: Whurr Publishers.

Couch, Arthur S. (1995) 'Anna Freud's adult psychoanalytic technique: a defence of classical analysis', *International Journal of Psycho-Analysis*, 76 (1): 153–71.

Durlak, J.A. (1979) 'Comparative effectiveness of paraprofessional and professional helpers', *Psychological Bulletin*, 86: 80–92.

Eigen, M. (1998) *The Psychoanalytic Mystic.* London: Free Association
Books.

Erikson, E. (1965) *Childhood and Society.* Harmondsworth: Penguin.

Fenichel, O. (1946) *The Psychoanalytic Theory of Neurosis.* London:
Routledge.

Fairbairn, W.R.D. (1994) *Psychoanalytic Studies of the Personality.* London:
Routledge.

Fordham, F. (1953) *An Introduction to Jung's Psychology.* Harmondsworth:
Penguin.

Fordham, M. (1974) 'Countertransference and technique', in M. Fordham, R.
Gordon, J. Hubback and K. Lambert (eds), *Technique in Jungian Analysis.*
London: Heinemann.

Freud, A. (1968) *The Ego and the Mechanisms of Defence.* London: Hogarth
Press.

Freud, A. (1973) *Normality and Pathology in Childhood.* London: Penguin.

Freud, S. (1905) *Three Essays on the Theory of Sexuality.* Penguin Freud
Library, Volume 7. London: Penguin.

Freud, S. (1913) *On Beginning the Treatment.* Standard Edition, Volume XII.
London: Hogarth Press.

Freud, S. (1914) *Remembering, Repeating and Working Through.* Standard
Edition, Volume XII. London: Hogarth Press.

Freud, S. (1920) *Beyond the Pleasure Principle.* Penguin Freud Library,
Volume 11. London: Penguin.

Freud, S. (1937) *Analysis Terminable and Interminable.* Standard Edition,
Volume XXIII. London: Hogarth Press.

Freud, S. (1940) *An Outline of Psychoanalysis.* Penguin Freud Library, Volume
15. London: Penguin.

Freud, S. and Breuer, J. (1895) *Studies on Hysteria.* Penguin Freud Library,
Volume 3. London: Penguin.

Fromm, E. (1959) *Sigmund Freud's Mission.* New York: Harper and Bros.

Fromm, E. (1967) *Psychoanalysis and Religion.* New Haven, CT: Yale
University Press.

Goetz, B. (1975) 'That is all I have to say about Freud: Bruno Goetz's remi-
niscences of Sigmund Freud'. *International Review of Psycho-Analysis.* 2,
139–43.

Gomez, L. (1996) *An Introduction to Object Relations.* London: Free
Association Books.

Gosling, R. (1968) 'What is transference?', in J. Sutherland, (ed.), *The*

Psychoanalytic Approach. London: Baillière, Tindall and Cassell.

Grant, B. (1984) 'Fitness for community: a response to Langs and Kohut', *Journal of Pastoral Care,* 38 (4): 324–37.

Greenberg, J.R. and Mitchell, S.A. (1983) *Object Relations in Psychoanalytic Theory.* London: Harvard University Press.

Greenson, R.R. (1967) *The Technique and Practice of Psychoanalysis, Volume 1.* London: Hogarth Press.

Guntrip, H. (1961) *Personality Structure and Human Interaction.* London: Hogarth Press.

Guntrip, H. (1968) *Schizoid Phenomena, Object Relations and the Self.* London: Hogarth Press.

Guntrip, H. (1971) *Psychoanalytic Theory, Therapy and the Self.* London: Hogarth Press.

Guntrip, H. (1975) 'My experience of analysis with Fairbairn and Winnicott', *International Journal of Psycho-Analysis*, 2: 145–56.

Hartung, B. (1979) 'The capacity to enter latency in learning pastoral psychotherapy', *Journal of Supervision and Training in Ministry* (Chicago, IL), 2: 46–59.

Hill, J. (1993) 'Am I a Kleinian? Is anyone?', *British Journal of Psychotherapy*, 9 (4): 463–75.

Holmes, J. (1993) *John Bowlby and Attachment Theory.* London: Routledge.

Jacobs, M. (1992) *Sigmund Freud.* London: Sage Publications.

Jacobs, M. (1993a) *Living Illusions: a Psychology of Belief.* London: SPCK.

Jacobs, M. (1993b) *Still Small Voice: an Introduction to Pastoral Counselling.* London: SPCK.

Jacobs, M. (1994) 'Psychodynamic counselling – identity achieved?', *Journal of Psychodynamic Counselling*, 1 (1): 79–92.

Jacobs, M. (1995) *D. W. Winnicott.* London: Sage Publications.

Jacobs, M. (ed.) (1996a) *In Search of Supervision.* Buckingham: Open University Press.

Jacobs, M. (1996b) 'Parallel process – confirmation and critique', *Journal of Psychodynamic Counselling*, 2 (1): 55–66.

Jacobs, M. (1996c) 'Suitable clients for counselling and psychotherapy', *Self and Society*, 24 (5): 3–7.

Jacobs, M. (1998) *The Presenting Past: the Core of Psychodynamic Counselling and Therapy* (revised and enlarged edition). Buckingham: Open University Press.

Jacobs, M. (1999) *Swift to Hear* (2nd enlarged edition). London: SPCK.

Kennedy, E. and Charles, S. (1989) *On Becoming a Counsellor* (2nd edition). Dublin: Gill and Macmillan.

165

Keppen, J. (1985) *Beyond Freud: a Study of Modern Psychoanalytic Theorists.* Hillsdale, NJ: The Analytic Press.

Kernberg, O. (1975) *Borderline Conditions and Pathological Narcissism.* New York: Jason Aronson.

Klein, J. (1987) *Our Need for Others and Its Roots in Infancy.* London: Routledge.

Kohon, G. (ed.) (1986) *The British School of Psychoanalysis: the Independent Tradition.* London: Free Association Books.

Kohut, H. (1971) *The Analysis of the Self.* London: Hogarth Press.

Kohut, H. (1977) *The Restoration of the Self.* New York: International Universities Press.

Kotowicz, Z. (1997) *R.D. Laing and the Paths of Anti-Psychiatry.* London: Routledge.

Kübler-Ross, E. (1970) O*n Death and Dying.* London: Tavistock.

Laing, R.D. (1965) *The Divided Self.* Harmondsworth: Penguin.

Langs, R. (1978) *The Listening Process.* New York: Jason Aronson.

Little, M.I. (1985) 'Winnicott working in areas where psychotic anxieties predominate: a personal record'. *Free Associations*, 3: 9–42.

Lomas, P. (1973) *True and False Experience.* London: Allen Lane.

Lomas, P. (1981) *The Case for a Personal Psychotherapy.* Oxford: Oxford University Press. (2nd edition, 1993, under a new title, *The Psychotherapy of Everyday Life.* London and New Brunswick: Transaction Publishers.)

Lomas, P. (1987) *The Limits of Interpretation.* London: Penguin.

Malan, D.H. (1976) *Toward the Validation of Psychodynamic Psychotherapy.* New York: Plenum Medical Book Co.

Malan, D.H. (1979) *Individual Psychotherapy and the Science of Psychodynamics.* London: Butterworth.

Malan, D.H. and Osimo, F. (1992) *Psychodynamics, Training and Outcome in Brief Psychotherapy*. Oxford: Butterworth/Heinemann.

Maroda, K. (1991) *The Power of Countertransference: Innovation in Analytic Technique.* Chichester: John Wiley.

Mearns, D. and Thorne, B. (1988) *Person-Centred Counselling in Action.* London: Sage Publications.

Molnos, A. (1995) *A Question of Time: Essentials of Brief Dynamic Psychotherapy.* London: Karnac Books.

Monger, J. (1998) 'The gap between theory and practice: a consideration of the fee', *Journal of Psychodynamic Counselling*', 4 (1): 93–106.

Parkes, C.M. (1972) *Bereavement.* Harmondsworth: Penguin.

Racker, H. (1968) *Transference and Countertransference.* London: Hogarth Press.

Rayner, E. (1990) *The Independent Mind in British Psychoanalysis.* London: Free Association Books.

Roazen, P. (1979) *Freud and His Followers.* Harmondsworth: Penguin.

Rubins, J.L. (1978) *Karen Horney.* London: Weidenfeld and Nicolson.

Rycroft, C. (1985) *Psychoanalysis and Beyond.* London: Chatto and Windus.

Samuels, A. (1985) *Jung and the Post-Jungians.* London: Routledge and Kegan Paul.

Sandler, J. (1976) in J. Naiman, 'Panel on the fundamentals of psychic change in clinical practice', *International Journal of Psychoanalysis*, 57: 411–17.

Searles, H. (1955) 'The informational value of the supervisor's emotional experiences', in H. Searles (1965), *Collected Papers on Schizophrenia and Related Subjects.* London: Hogarth Press.

Searles, H. (1979) *Counter-transference and Related Subjects.* New York: International Universities Press.

Segal, J. (1992) *Melanie Klein.* London: Sage Publications.

Shelley, C. (ed.) (1998) *The Psychotherapies and Homosexualities.* London: Free Association Books.

Sills, C. (ed.) (1997) *Contracts in Counselling.* London: Sage Publications.

Singer, E. (1965) *Key Concepts in Psychotherapy.* New York: Random House.

Smith, D.L. (1991) *Hidden Conversations – an Introduction to Communicative Psychoanalysis.* London: Routledge.

Stewart, I. (1989) *Transactional Analysis Counselling in Action.* London: Sage Publications.

Sullivan, E.M. (ed.) (1998) *Unconscious Communication in Practice.* Buckingham: Open University Press.

Sutherland, J.D. (1989) *Fairbairn's Journey into the Interior.* London: Free Association Books.

Symington, J. and Symington, N. (1996) *The Clinical Thinking of Wilfred Bion.* London: Routledge.

Symington, N. (1994) *Emotion and Spirit.* London: SPCK.

Walker, M. (ed.) (1995) *Morag – Myself or Mother Hen?* Buckingham: Open University Press.

Winnicott, D.W. (1958) *Collected Papers: Through Paediatrics to Psycho-analysis.* London: Hogarth Press.

Winnicott, D.W. (1960) 'Counter-transference', in D.W. Winnicott (1965), *The Maturational Processes and the Facilitating Environment: Studies in the Theory of Emotional Development.* London: Hogarth Press.

Winnicott, D.W. (1964) *The Child, the Family and the Outside World.* Harmondsworth: Penguin.

Winnicott, D.W. (1965) *The Maturational Processes and the Facilitating Environment: Studies in the Theory of Emotional Development.* London: Hogarth Press.

Winnicott, D.W. (1971) *Playing and Reality.* London: Routledge.

Wolff, H.H. (1977) 'Loss: a central theme in psychotherapy', *British Journal of Psychology,* 50: 11–19.

Index

guidance, 18
guilt, 86, 101, 106
Guntrip, H., 3, 115, 118, 119, 135

Hannah, xii, 1–2, 3, 9, 11, 13, 15,
    17, 18, 19, 20, 21, 22, 24–5, 26,
    27, 31, 32, 34, 36, 37, 38, 39, 40,
    41–2, 43, 44, 45, 46, 47, 52,
    53–63, 75, 76, 77–8, 80, 81,
    83–5, 87, 99, 104, 106, 110–13,
    127, 131, 132, 138–46, 151, 152,
    155, 159
Hartung, B. 117
hate, 9, 126
    see also aggression
here-and-now, 19, 26, 81
Hill, J., 115
history, client's, 14, 28, 40, 42
history-taking, 28, 40, 41
holidays, see breaks in counselling
Holmes, J., 3
homosexuality, 131
Horney, K., 3
humanistic therapy, 35, 115, 135, 148
hypotheses, 53, 58, 75
hypnosis, 10

id, 7, 11–12
idealisation, 32, 101, 103, 106, 108,
    119, 137
identification, 102, 104, 137
identifying with the client, 37
illness, counsellor's, see breaks in
    counselling
illusions, giving up, 148–9
immediacy, 15–16
incest, 112
independent school
    (psychoanalysis), 3–4
individual psychology, see Adlerian
    counselling
individuation process, 137
inhibitions, 51
insight, 28, 44, 45, 66, 69, 70, 79,
    129, 133, 155, 156

instincts, see drives
instruction, 45
integrative counsellors/therapists, 6
integrative therapy, 115
intellectualisation, 66, 68, 101, 105,
    108
internal objects, 6–8, 9, 15, 18, 88
    see also internal world
internal world, 15, 18, 22, 33, 156
internalisation of counsellor, 88,
    156
interpretations, 19, 35, 40, 43–5, 48,
    60, 67, 71, 74, 78, 80, 91, 103,
    109–13, 114, 118, 124, 127–8,
    129–30, 138, 140, 141, 145, 149,
    154, 156, 157
interruptions, 31, 34
interventions, 62–3, 79, 117, 129;
    timing of, 79, 129
introjection, 101–102, 104
intuition, 137
isolation, 101, 105, 106

Jacobs, M., 3, 4, 6, 7, 10, 14, 21, 35,
    64, 65, 75, 107, 115, 131, 161,
    132, 138
Journal of Psychodynamic
    Counselling, 161
Jung, C., 3, 4, 5, 7, 137, 162
Jungians, 4, 5, 137

Kafka, F., 93
Karl, xii, 29–31, 32, 36, 37, 38, 40,
    44, 45, 52, 61, 72–4, 75, 76, 78,
    79, 85, 92–4, 98, 99, 101, 102,
    105, 106, 107, 109–10, 117,
    120–1, 123, 124–5, 147, 150–1,
    157–9
Kennedy, E., 109, 118
Kernberg, O., 3
Klein, J., 4, 162
Klein, M., 3, 4, 5
Kleinians, 3, 4, 5, 7, 8, 115, 137
Kohon, G., 4
Kohut, H., 3